A Rose for Tomorrow:
Biography of Frederick C. Schreiber

Jerome D. Schein

ISBN 0-913072-46-X

Published by
National Association of the Deaf
814 Thayer Avenue
Silver Spring, MD 20910

All royalties arising from the sale of this book have been donated by the author to the Frederick C. Schreiber Memorial Fund.

Preface

Y ou turn and see a magnificent sunset: splashes of fiery orange against a vivid blue sky. You feel shaken—awestruck, excited, ecstatic. Strong emotions play against a single thought: you wish you could preserve this fabulous moment. You want to capture it somehow, so that later you can rekindle this brush against the cosmos. You want time to contemplate, to try to understand the way it affects you. Somehow you cannot. Even as you watch, the colors fade, the sky darkens, night erases the scene.

For many people, Fred Schreiber's life resembles a brilliant sunset. They would like to hold onto his presence, the magnificent color of his life. They wish they could rekindle the flame he lit in them. They miss his affection, his humor, his inspiration. Like a sunset, his life has been too evanescent, too strong to be kept for long. Still, this book will try to preserve some of the meaning of his life, even if that spirit must inevitably escape. This book aims to tell his story. It marks his passage through our time. A remarkable passage.

A book for Fred will seem right to those who knew him. They may want to add to its pages one more facet of this complex man's character, to tell still another story about him, to preserve yet another anecdote. They may feel the book does not do him justice. But the necessity for telling his story—that will not, for them, need justification.

Those who have not met Fred may wonder why he deserves a biography. His achievements give the answer. He was a builder, a creator, a man who added good to the world he found. He altered the flow of history; he changed for the better the society in which he lived. Any decent account of his life—and this book tries to be that—proclaims his worth.

How to tell his story? The plan is simple: First a biographical sketch. Next, his collected papers. Then his honors, awards from organizations, and tributes from his friends.

The biography sets the scene, but the best telling about him comes from his own words. Throughout the account of his mature years, quotes from his writings are inserted to punctuate events. He has left us an extensive written record of his thoughts and actions. He was prolific. Throughout his years as Executive Secretary of the National Association of the Deaf, he seldom failed to write his administration's record which he called "Home Office Notes." Perhaps his best thoughts can be found in his speeches; he made hundreds. Unfortunately, no Boswell followed him about to record his impromptu remarks, and he was careless of his own productions. Many of his scripts have disappeared. Enough remain, however, to present his basic themes and to reveal his characteristic style.

How his life affected those around him tells best in their own words. So many words have been spoken about Fred that choosing among them is difficult. The selection of tributes, comments and memorials will, it is hoped, convey the great breadth of his influence and the deep, warm emotions he stirred in so many people.

Assembling the pieces of Fred's life has taken much assistance from those around him. The essential aid and encouragement has come from many people who will forgive me, I pray, if I only mention a few: Elizabeth DeMarco, Edward C. Carney, Edith Kleberg, and Harold Schwartz. The new Executive Director, Albert Pimentel, has been unswerving in his support for this project.

Kathleen Schreiber—Kit—has tolerated my intrusions into the magnificent life she shared with Fred. She has winced at my clumsy interpretations, corrected blatant errors, and even wrote out anecdotes too delicate to entrust to retelling. Like her husband, Kit deserves a better book. But like Fred, she is aware of the shortcomings of others and she most graciously accepts that which is offered with love.

A last prefatory note. What about the title *A Rose for Tomorrow?* Fred had a passion for roses—not to have or see or smell, but to grow. He delighted in their beauty. So at his memorial, roses provided a poignant and fitting symbol. The rose signifies Fred's love for, and his gifts to, others. He planted roses to improve everyone's view, to perfume the air for all of us.

Why *for Tomorrow?* Because Fred was unselfish. He struggled for ideals. He fought for others. He gave himself to great causes. He worked for, protected, and cherished those who were weak, disabled, disheartened. That is why the rose is for tomorrow. Fred planted for others to harvest. He did not live to enjoy the roses. Still, no one doubts he would go on planting roses—as he did—knowing they were not for him. Here, then, is *A Rose for Tomorrow.*

Abbreviations Used in Text

To assist the reader, the following abbreviations will be followed throughout Chapters I and II:

DA = *The Deaf American,* the present title of the National Association of the Deaf's magazine.

DCE = *Dee Cee Eyes,* publication of the District of Columbia Club of the Deaf.

HON = Home Office Notes, the title Fred used for his monthly report to the members. It appeared as a regular section of DA.

NAD = National Association of the Deaf

PG = Personal Glimpses, a paper written by Fred and given to a parent conference in Minneapolis, 6 May 1972.

SW = *The Silent Worker,* title of the NAD's magazine before its name changed to DA.

Quotations from DA, DCE, and SW are identified by the journal's abbreviation followed by the month, year, and page number. Thus, DA 10/78, 21 should be read as "Deaf American for October, 1978, page 21."

Table of Contents

Frederick C. Schreiber 1922–1979

Chapter I
Biography up to 1966

After 1965, the history of deafness in the United States cannot be properly written without consideration of Frederick Carl Schreiber. The same could be said with almost equal force about the history of deafness in the world, for his influence spread far beyond his country's borders. He brought his rare qualities of leadership to bear on issues basic to securing the rights of all deaf people, regardless of their nationality.

So great has been his influence, so vast his accomplishments, that he could easily be forgotten! People quickly become accustomed to a new status in society, and deaf people are probably no exception to this generalization. Once they are comfortable with what they have attained, many forget how they got there. So it is, also, with their leaders: people often forget the former leaders soon after the new ones take charge.

Fred might also be forgotten, because he avoided self aggrandizement. He was often in the spotlight, especially in his last few years. But he generously shared its light with others, constantly praising those around him and modestly acknowledging their roles, no matter how small. More importantly, as regarded many accomplishments, he saw no reason to thank anyone—or to be thanked. Deaf people had only gotten rights denied them for centuries. Thanks were not in order. What was appropriate was the joy of comrades who had succeeded in a good fight.

To understand Fred at all, then, we must review his life along with the recent history of the National Association of the Deaf (NAD). NAD, of course, stands at the center of the deaf world, so in recalling its history we are considering the history of deafness in the United States.

NAD was 42 when Fred was born. By the time Fred entered Gallaudet College, NAD had passed the half-century mark. Not until its 84th birthday did Fred assume the major leadership role in NAD. He died the year before NAD reached its centenary.

What was NAD like when Fred became its Executive Secretary?

The NAD in 1964–1965

Issues of *The Silent Worker* for 1964 and *The Deaf American* for 1965 contain material which clearly illustrate the NAD's status in those years. Two quotations make clear that other organizations, voluntary and government, did not regard NAD as *the* representative of deaf people—as almost all do today. In his monthly letter to the members, NAD President Byron B. Burnes writes,

> California has been the scene of a number of inspiring workshops during recent months . . . The first was a workshop for social workers which met in Berkeley. The NAD was not invited to this one but it was nation-wide in scope and reports are that its deliberations were stimulating. (SW 4/64, 21)

In reading that quotation, the reader may be interested to recall that NAD headquarters were in Berkeley, California at the time—the very city in which the meeting was held. Today, it would be shocking not to find NAD represented at any important national meeting concerned with deafness, regardless of its location.

A few months later the newly elected NAD President Robert G. Sanderson indicates the impending shift in the federal regard for the organization:

> It may be that we soon shall receive an invitation to appoint a representative to a very important committee near the top level of government. We hope it comes through in time for the next issue of our magazine. (DA 12/64, 21)

The invitation, which did arrive shortly thereafter, was to a seat on the President's Committee on Employment of the Handicapped.

NAD members express some harsh opinions in those transitional issues of SW. In reply to his request for evaluation of the organization by members of the Ways and Means Committee which he then headed, Sanderson receives a number of lengthy replies. Here are samples from three which appear in the same issue of SW:

> This is a difficult thing to do—evaluate a program which deals with the general welfare of the deaf in the economic and educational fields. About all that I can say is that you (the NAD) are just another stand-by organization. This is the same for state organizations and I am sure the average deaf person knows it and this. Why pay every year then? Why not only when the pocketbook is in danger? This is the main point in my feelings. For the NAD to become a dominant, dynamic force and spokesman of and for the deaf it must be capable of presenting and carrying out daring plans for the problems of the future.— Keith Lange, Oregon (SW 1/64, 14)

> The NAD must get closer to the deaf population. I realize that for years the NAD has been attempting to win more members, but most contacts with the average deaf person have been made on an effort to sell the NAD, but no effort has been made towards obtaining the opinion of this 'man on the street.' The NAD sends speakers to state conventions with the purpose of telling the states about the NAD, but is there any effort on the part of the speakers to feel the current, to probe the general sentiments?

And lastly, but most important, the NAD needs practical projects. We must have selling points to prove our worth to the deaf. I may sound materialistic, but don't you tell me that a materialistic project will not make the deaf sit up and listen. The NAD is frequently compared with the NAACP, but I would hate to make a comparison of what the NAD has done for the deaf with what the NAACP has done for the Negro. The NAD must help the deaf to secure better employment, it must help the deaf to secure a better education, it must help the deaf to take their proper place in society. In short, it must make America a more comfortable, and a more fair place for the deaf to live. More accurately perhaps, what we need is a crusade.— Harold Ramger, NAD Board Member (SW, 1/64, 14-15)

The Kansas Association voted to collect the quota with membership fees starting in 1964. It was also understood that the members would pay the 1963 and 1964 quotas to the treasurer. From my experience in trying to make this collection, I would say half the members did not attend the business meetings and knew nothing about it. They have been hard to convince that payment is to their advantage. Many have asked, 'Why should we pay that money to the NAD?' This I can answer. Then they ask, 'What has the NAD ever done to help the deaf in the various states in the past?' I am unable to tell them. I have no data on past help given by the NAD, only word of mouth, which may be rumor. I need PROOF.— Henry Yahn, Kansas (SW 1/64, 16)

The picture of discontent which Fred Schreiber faces on the eve of his assumption of an executive role in NAD is painfully clear. NAD, at age 84 years, has not earned the respect of the deaf population. Within a few short years, Fred changes all that. All alone? Of course not. But his leadership moves NAD from the political and social backwaters into the mainstream of deaf life. How he does it, how he guides that gigantic turnabout, is a fascinating story.

But first let us ask, how was Fred prepared for the role he played? Where did he learn to lead? Who taught him how to balance pressures from members and service providers? From what source did his administrative style emerge?

Birth to Age Six

Fred was born on February 1, 1922, in Brooklyn, New York. His parents, Helen and Louis Schreiber, already had a son, Harry. A few years after Fred's birth, his sister was born, completing the family—an average-sized family, by the standards of those years, and one free of any members with apparent physical disabilities.

Economically, the family positioned itself solidly in the middle class. Louis and Helen had emigrated to the United States from Czarist Russia in the great wave of immigrants at the turn of the century. By the time of Fred's arrival, his father had established himself as a businessman and his mother had thoroughly acclimated to her adopted country. Fred's family, like thousands of others, validated the metaphor of the melting pot.

Like his family, Fred was fairly typical as a young boy. Bright and notably mischievous, he suffered some injuries (a broken leg at three years of age) and the usual childhood illnesses. Then, in 1928, he had four successive bouts of spinal meningitis. The consequences proved physically devastating.

Deafness Descends

The repeated inflammations of whatever invasive organisms attacked his central nervous system left Fred deaf and crippled. To a group of parents he was addressing nearly half a century later, he nonchalantly described what happened:

> First of all, I lost my hearing at the age of 6½, as the result of recurring bouts of spinal meningitis. Actually, I am a medical freak and the case history of my battle with meningitis is recorded in the MEDICAL JOURNAL, but I won't tell you when, since women are not the only people who lie about their age. More importantly, the recurring battle with meningitis left me with a severe curvature of the spine which was straightened out by means of a plaster cast and several years of wearing a brace. (PG)

The plaster cast covered him from neck to knees. For a time, he could only be moved in a baby carriage. His regular schooling was interrupted. But he was not yet managed as a deaf child by his parents. Amazing as it may seem, Fred had not gained conscious awareness of his deafness. In his own words:

> During this period, I attended not a school for the deaf, but a school for crippled children. I must say that I was not aware that I was deaf. School was school, and because my teacher did not move around the room the way teachers do in public schools, I had no difficulty in understanding her and did very well as far as academics were concerned. But an adjunct to a school for crippled children was the school bus, which I detested because it picked me up early in the morning and brought me home late in the afternoon, so late that it cut into whatever time I might have to play and all I really wanted was to go back to public school.

> Finally, the brace was removed and I pestered my family to let me go back to the neighborhood school. At that time I was nine-years-old and presumably had been deaf for at least two years. Nevertheless, I was still in the dark; a situation that must appear unbelievable to you. But all I can remember of this period was going from doctor to doctor, who waved tuning forks in front of my ears and persisted in hitting my knees with rubber hammers. All of which were quite uncomprehensible to a nine-year-old. However, if that was what it took to get out of a school for crippled children and back to public school, I was all for it. Finally, I was permitted to return to public school, and, immediately, I was in trouble. First it was in the schoolyard. As many of you know, children then, if not now, used to assemble in the schoolyard to talk, play and wait for time to go to class. It seemed that everyone knew when it was time to drop everything and line up for classes—everyone but I. I don't mind admitting that it was a real puzzle, and one that bugged me for many years afterward. However, I would have died before I would ask a classmate, 'How come you know when to get in line and I don't?' In the classroom itself, the problem was the same. So long as the teacher remained where I could see her, I could understand, but once she moved out of my range of vision I was lost. This happened repeatedly; there were problems when she would say 'Fred, now you.' And I was thoroughly bewildered until it turned out we were reading aloud and someone had just finished a paragraph. So I had to be shown where the last reader left off so I could begin.

4

What I am trying to say is that I never knew what was wrong. I learned to lip read, if that is the correct way of expressing it, without ever having a lesson in my life, and I suffered continual embarrassment simply because I had no idea what was the matter with me. Sure, there were times when I was out in the street playing and a playmate might say, 'Your mother's calling you.' However, this did not really bother me; no kid ever heard his mother calling him, why should I be the exception? There were also times when my father might say, 'Shh, I'm listening to the radio.' But at those times, I was apparently too hurt to ever stop to wonder why I hadn't heard the radio. And the reason, as I later found out, that I never was told about my hearing loss was that my parents were advised to treat me as if I were 'normal'. But this also helps to illustrate why so many people claim lip reading is an art, and either you have it or you don't. (PG)

It should not be difficult for the reader to understand why Fred did not like to discuss those difficult years. When he did talk about them, he used his experiences to explain deafness to the unafflicted: "I think some of the things that have happened to me may be of value, if not in dealing with your own children, in understanding why the NAD and many of the deaf people take the positions they do in relation to education and employment, in connection with methodology, and our feelings concerning speech and speech reading." He said the latter at the same conference of parents of deaf children, in Minneapolis (PG). Wherever he met parents, he aroused their hopes. He was a son of whom any parent would be proud. He was open to them, not critical. He had gone through a lot, but he was not bitter. When parents of deaf children saw the struggling child in him now grown to a fine man, their expectations for their deaf children soared.

Learning to Be Deaf

In 1932, at age 10, Fred entered a school with other deaf children. There the awareness of his deafness grew. But also, Fred realized that having heard for his first six years he had a tremendous advantage in language development over his born-deaf contemporaries. Let him tell it:

From public school, I went to the Lexington School for the Deaf, one of the better oral schools in this country. I did not know how to use sign language; in fact, I was not even aware that deaf children could not speak or had to be taught to do this. All I knew at the time was that I could not hear and I was in a residential school full of the most weird characters you ever saw. I learned fingerspelling at Lexington; I also noted that learning there was a tedious process, with my teachers repeating words and sentences over and over again, boring me to tears because *I* understood them the first time. It did not make much sense, but what does a ten-year-old do in those circumstances? At any rate, it became obvious that my language and speech were far superior to those of my classmates, and in my second year at the school, I began to understand something, particularly the advantages I had as a post-lingually deafened student over my prelingually deaf classmates. And I resented the fact that my teachers were taking advantages of this. At any rate, a change in school policy resulted in all the boys at the Lexington School being transferred to the New York School for the Deaf, then and now, called Fanwood. This school was not denigrated exactly, at Lexington, but we did get some real horror tales about it. Included was the story that students at Fanwood had to remain until they were 21. As an 8th-grade student, the prospect of remaining in the 8th grade for the next eight years was appalling, but it was either Fanwood or back to the school-bus bit, and I preferred Fanwood to school buses. Fanwood used the simultaneous method, and it was there that I got my first taste of what could be done when there was ease of communication, and it was there that I learned about Gallaudet College, which offered at least the prospect of escaping from remaining in the 8th grade for the next eight years. I will confess that I had no burning desire to go to college; I was motivated strictly to getting out of school. I do not mean to imply that Fanwood was a bad school, or that there was anything about the school that was responsible for my wanting to leave. To the contrary, the administration, my teachers, the principal, everyone was helpful, kind and dedicated—I was just tired of school. (PG)

Fred neglects to say that he first tried to leave Fanwood when he was 14 years old. His family and the school refused to permit him to graduate. He spent the next year in a college preparatory program at Fanwood, after which he was accepted at Gallaudet College, the only institution of higher education in the world at that time devoted exclusively to deaf students. The college was 71 years old when Fred entered it. He was 15!

Higher Education

Fred found his intellectual peers at Gallaudet College. The college enrolled fewer than 200 deaf students, choosing as a matter of President Percival Hall's policy to accept only the intellectual elite among the deaf schoolage population. Despite his comparative youth, Fred easily competed academically. In five years—the college curriculum included a preparatory year then as now—he earned a bachelor's degree in chemistry, a major field he regarded as the least undesirable of the generally unappealing, for him, options.

Socially, Fred also fared well. He edited a humorous column, "The Hurdy Gurdy," in the college newspaper. From all available accounts, he was popular with both sexes. He did have some small difficulty with the administration, a prophetic clash with authority. Pamela Luft recounts this story Fred told her about his college days:

> Fred entered Gallaudet believing that college was a place to express oneself without fear of reprisal, in an atmosphere of academic freedom. Consequently, he spoke his mind: as a result he immediately got into trouble, a condition that continued throughout the five years he was at Gallaudet. In one instance, the dean of women objected to his fraternity's plan to dim the lights at an upcoming dance. In reply, Fred said she should take her mind out of the gutter. The college president heard of the incident and instructed Fred to apologize to the dean. Refusing to be so humiliated and compromised, Fred told the dean he was sorry for what he had said earlier—she could certainly leave her mind in the gutter if she wished. (DA 12/76, 11-12)

Fred had a Lincolnesque build—tall (nearly six feet), dark complexioned, bony. At Gallaudet College he kept his hair closely cropped in a crew cut. When it grew out, his hair curled and fought his comb. Photographs from his college days show a neatly dressed, severe-looking young man. Most of the time, however, Fred dressed casually—some even considered him careless of his clothing, an impression he sustained

6

throughout his life. But that impression quickly receded for those who got to know him and was replaced by the strength and vigor of his expression, his unfailing humor, and the rapid movements of his long, thin fingers. Fred looked exciting, approachable, uncomplicated, yet interesting. He looked friendly.

He kept as active physically as intellectually. He bowled, fenced, wrestled, played tennis. He was not a "star" performer, but he was enthusiastic. Opponents might overcome Fred, but they knew they had been in a good contest. His college yearbook, *The Tower Clock*, carries this legend beneath his photograph:

'Alas, from what high hope to what relapse, Unlook'd for are we fallen.' 'Ferdie' is the ladies' man of the class, as well as being quite an enigma. A New Yorker in manners, a genius in the class room, a book lover, and a play boy, he has studied less than any other student, yet has done well with his grades. If he ever settles down he will make a fine man. Kappa Gamma Fraternity 1941–42; Kappa Gamma Officer 1941–42; Buff and Blue Board 1940–42; Wrestling Manager 1941–42; Member, ETA BETA SIGMA 1940–42; President, ETA BETA SIGMA 1941–42; Editor-in-chief, Tower Clock 1941–42.

Graduation, in 1942, found the United States in the midst of World War II. Fred had entered Gallaudet College during the closing days of economic depression. Now he emerged, with diploma, into an even grimmer period of United States history. The national plight had a tragic counterpart in his family; his father fell ill and lost his sight and his business. The gay college atmosphere abruptly terminated for Fred. The circumstances demanded courage, and Fred had it.

The War Years

Deaf people established outstanding production records in munitions plants during World War II. Fred was among them. He went to Akron, Ohio, where he took a machine-tending job at the Firestone plant. He was ambitious, and he began to climb the industrial ladder, moving to better-paid, more-demanding jobs within Firestone. In that ascent, he encountered discrimination. He dealt with negative prejudice against himself then in the same way as he would later fight prejudice against other deaf people—with intelligence, persistence, and, above all, humor.

As I mentioned before, deaf workers had been actively recruited for Firestone and Goodyear. We were not there as a gesture on the part of these companies—they wanted us, and they went out to get us. But when I decided that I would remain in Akron for the duration of the war, and started looking around for a better job within the company, I got a flat turn down. Being aware that an able-bodied, draft-exempt male was highly desired on the labor market, I demanded a chance to prove my worth or I would quit. So this time I got a runaround. While this is a long story, I will make it short and just say that I finally got promoted and became a machine-shop inspector where it quickly became apparent that my deafness was an asset rather than a liability. Machinists on piecework operations had a tendency to argue with inspectors when their work was rejected and how do you argue with an inspector who can't hear you and who needed but to look away to render one impotently defending his work? At any rate, at the end of the war, I became what might be called in industry, a 'gate crasher,' which is to say I was placed in departments at Firestone where no deaf workers had ever been hired, to see if it were possible for deaf people to work in these areas. It was hard, and it was challenging, and you might say I have been doing this ever since. (PG)

The four years in Akron made Fred increasingly aware of deaf adults who were much less capable than his college friends. Those years also opened his eyes to the deaf community's problems. With so many deaf workers crowding into Akron, the local deaf club flourished. It was an essential gathering place, the center of deaf social activities. Most naturally, it attracted Fred.

He learned about the controversy between those who favored using sign language in the education of deaf children and those who opposed sign. Orally proficient himself, Fred nonetheless sided with the signers, especially against deaf persons who grew up in an oral environment and urged its virtues on all deaf people. "The idea of a person having experienced only oral education and insisting it is best," he reasoned, "is akin to a person having only tasted grapefruit, but doggedly insisting it tastes better than oranges although he has never tasted an orange". (DCE 5/60, 1)

Thirty years later Fred continued to debate with oral deaf adults. An exchange of correspondence with Dr. Latham Breunig, former president of the Oral Deaf Adult Society of the Alexander Graham Bell Association, appeared in DA shortly before Fred's death. Reading the letters, one can imagine the youthful Schreiber responding to the familiar arguments, making the same counter points he had made in the Akron clubrooms.

Fred encountered another aspect of discrimination, one for which he developed a ploy he continued to use after Akron. He found society valued speech so highly that those who did not speak paid heavy economic penalties. Similarly, those who were poor speechreaders met stubborn prejudice by some employers:

I had the occasion to meet a woman who complained of her inability to secure employment because when she was interviewed, and asked if she could read lips, she said no. So I suggested to her, 'The next time you apply for a job, and are asked that question, you say, Yes—if you speak plain.' And it worked. She has been successfully employed for the past 10 years. She can't lipread any better than she could before, but now her employer thinks it is *his* fault!(PG)

Becoming deaf had not destroyed Fred's perspective. He did not react by forming an unreasoning view of deaf people as demigods or of hearing people as demons. For Fred, people remained people, fallible and worthwhile and lovable. He discovered that an effective argument to use against those who tried to impose their ways on others was simply to confront them with their own errors, their own weaknesses. He turned the accusations of those who blamed the deaf person for being different back on themselves. As he found in Akron, it worked.

Personally, the Akron years saw Fred pursuing a frenetic schedule. He and Kathleen Bedard worked seven days a week. Yet, they found time to go horseback riding almost every morning, driving to the stables in Fred's ancient Oldsmobile that used a can opener for a key and had a horrible shimmy whenever they hit a bump in the road (which was frequently). When it was finally reduced to the necessity of hammering on a wheel every five miles to keep it going, it was replaced with a fire-engine-red Pontiac convertible. Evenings were filled with club meetings, cards, socializing, until time to report for that graveyard shift. This pace continued through to their marriage and until Kathleen was put on maternity leave because of the ether used in the paint spray in the Aircraft division at Firestone.

Fred Founds a Family

Success in industry, during his Akron days, led Fred to consider marriage. He first met Kathleen (Kit) Bedard at Gallaudet College. She was a preparatory student and he was a senior assigned to tutor her. They met again at the club in Akron where both were active members.

As Fred told the story, he never proposed to Kit—his father did! In the summer of 1944, Kit and Fred went to New York City to meet Fred's parents. Louis Schreiber took it for granted that his son intended to marry Kit, so he, not Fred, initiated the discussion of wedding plans.

The marriage took place September 23, 1944. To satisfy Fred's parents, the bride and groom agreed to have their union blessed by a rabbi, though Kit was Catholic and Fred indifferent. Formal religion played an insignificant role in their marriage—a marriage that lasted thirty-five years. They celebrated holidays, like Christmas and Passover, as festivals, as family occasions rather than religious observances.

Their first child, Beverly Ann, was born August 21, 1945, while they still resided in Akron. Nearly four years elapsed before Louis George arrived on March 7, 1949. He and his brother Stephen Robert were born in New York City, the latter almost exactly one year later, March 5, 1950. Elizabeth Jean, the youngest, joined the family in Washington, D.C., February 25, 1954.

Reflecting on Fred's heavy involvement in the affairs of the deaf community while holding various full-time jobs, one might conclude Fred gave little time to his family. His children did not see it that way. Their devotion to their father came from mutual love and respect. He made time for them; he cared for them deeply.

His children could easily have been in awe of Fred, especially in later years when honors were heaped on him. He would not have it that way. He led them in laughter at his idiosyncrasies. He encouraged them to speak out, think independently, and mature. They shared his great adventure in deafness. He told them when he was worried and when he was elated. He and Kit made a family, and they kept the family together.

Perhaps more than anything else, Fred's irrepressible humor aided him in parenting. He had a fine sense of the ridiculous which prevented him from being pompous and overbearing, not just with his children but with anyone. At his memorial service, the deep impression his sense of humor had made pervaded the individual recollections.

Another characteristic that endeared him to his family was his generosity. Fred had to work hard for economic independence. He grew up in the Great Depression of the Thirties. Yet his willingness to share whatever he had—goods and ideas—was constantly before his children. They saw him invite strangers, acquaintances, friends to live with them. Some stayed for years. No terms, no constraints: the friend needed a place to stay and the Schreibers had room. Simple as that. Certainly, he lectured his children on "the value of a dollar," chided them for wastefulness, preached the virtues of thrift and hard work. But such precepts never obscured from them their father's essential generosity. They never doubted that he would share with them whatever he had. He always did.

The NAD in 1946

The nineteenth NAD convention met in Los Angeles, in 1940. Because of interstate travel restrictions imposed after Pearl Harbor, the next convention was postponed until 1946, in Louisville, Kentucky. It was convened by Dr. Tom L. Anderson, of Iowa, who had been elected president at the Los Angeles convention. Anderson had presided over NAD's war efforts, which included raising a Victory Fund. The $8,000 collected from the members purchased three Red Cross "Clubmobiles" used in Europe. NAD participated in a study of Gallaudet College, in opposition to a suit to revoke a deaf driver's license because of his deafness, and in the National Rehabilitation Advisory Council.

The Kentucky conventioneers heard, among others, a speech by Tom Dillon, "Why Schools for the Deaf Should Have More Deaf Principals." Dillon's proposal, by its modesty, reflected the era: what was urged was not more deaf *superintendents* but more *principals,* the second-echelon of school administrator. At the convention's conclusion, Byron B. Burnes accepted the presidency, a position he would hold until 1964.

The 1949 NAD Convention

Cleveland hosted the twenty-first convention, in 1949. Several notable features distinguished that meeting. The convention voted out all racial discrimination; henceforth, membership was open to all deaf persons, regardless of their skin color. The delegates heard about the organization's need for a permanent site and a full-time staff. Neither was established, but the issues were raised. *The Silent Worker,* the NAD's defunct periodical, was restored.

Fred attended that convention—his first. All three of its major developments were congenial to him. He was a civil libertarian, a believer in equal rights for all, not privileges for himself alone. His earlier bout with what he perceived to be administrative oppression in college presaged his later defense of weaker persons. Though the Cleveland assembly did not vote for a permanent home office, it planted the seed which sprouted 15 years later. During that decade and a half, Fred persistently watered and cultivated the soil holding that seed. Revival of *The Silent Worker* (now called *The Deaf American*) also suited Fred's working style. He understood at an early age the criticality of communication in binding together people. In college he wrote a column for the student newspaper. He edited the District of Columbia Club of the Deaf's newsletter when he returned to Washington, D.C., in 1952. And he never neglected "Home Office Notes", the column in DA that he began to write soon after becoming NAD's executive secretary. (In 15 years he only missed writing four columns, each time due to severe illness.)

In an interview years later, Fred discussed his attendance at the 1949 convention (DA 12/76, 10). He found too many of the delegates uninformed about the issues. Emerging from his exciting Akron experiences, Fred came to Cleveland eager to see the same kind of barrier-surmounting activities extended to the national level. In college he had first learned about the NAD. Now, in Cleveland, he held lofty expectations. The convention itself disappointed him, but it did not discourage him. In a few years he would lead the campaign to move the NAD into permanent quarters staffed with full-time personnel. The Cleveland convention exposed the impotence of part-time, unprofessional leadership.

Akron to Brooklyn

Fred's father died suddenly from a massive brain hemorrhage. Kathleen and daughter, Beverly, were sent to keep his mother company. Fred was dissatisfied with Akron and his new job in the tire plant that paid mediocre wages. He was also frustrated in his attempt to convince the older deaf residents that they should buy the old YMCA for a clubhouse. They had balked at the idea during the war when it was going for peanuts. The price had risen since the end of the war, and they were even more hesitant as they saw deaf workers departing. He could not stand their indecision in spite of all the arguments he put up. (Later years proved him right, but did not make the pill any less bitter.)

Fred remained at Firestone's plant, in Akron, until 1947. World War II having come to an end and munitions production having been cut back, Fred decided to take up teaching, the path on which he was headed when detoured by the war. He accepted a position, in Austin, at the Texas School for the Deaf. Like most deaf teachers, he was assigned to the secondary department where signing in the classroom was permissible. He stayed only a year, leaving after clashing with the school's administration over a policy he felt unfairly discriminated against married faculty members. Fred's idealism derailed his professional advancement. If he regretted his stand against what he saw as tyranny, he never said so.

From Austin, Fred travelled back to New York City. There, like many deaf men before him, he sought and obtained "his card"—the International Typographer's Union membership. As a union printer, Fred was able to earn a good living, though doing work which took little advantage of his considerable intellectual endowment or of his college education.

A great change in Fred's philosophy occurred in the summer of 1948. In Akron, the problems of poorly educated deaf adults had aroused his sympathy. But he did not empathize with them. Their problems, he believed, came from their lack of English language skills. The solution was obvious. If only they could read English better, write English better, speak English better, they would have fewer difficulties at work and in the community.

Fred volunteered as a tutor of uneducated deaf applicants of the New York State Office of Vocational Rehabilitation. For almost three years he devoted himself to this taxing labor in his free time. He added greatly to his understanding of less capable deaf adults and developed an affection for them that persisted for the rest of his life.

A deaf couple lived on the block adjoining his mother's house. The husband was an Italian immigrant with broken English punctuated with eloquent gestures more beautiful than any words. One evening he stopped by to ask Fred to come to the Brooklyn Association of the Deaf with him. At this time, it was a men's club and women went only occasionally as guests at special affairs. There Fred met one of the finest cooks in town, one who knew how to make pastrami, corned beef, and roast beef in the best Jewish tradition, yet who knew only about 100 words of English. There, also, he met other deaf people from Hungary, France, Germany, Holland, and many home-grown locals. They welcomed him to their club, toasted him, and told him stories of their experiences in Europe and America. Fred returned home late after that evening very subdued. When Kathleen asked him what was wrong, he looked up and said almost with awe, "You don't need English to be smart. They didn't even have to tell me that—they showed me!"

Fred was indifferent to the oral-manual controversy until he became a private tutor for the New York Department of Vocational Rehabilitation. His first pupil was a deaf boy with very bad vision who had attended an oral school for over ten years and never even learned to write his name. Fred's frustration with the young man had its hilarious moments. The neighbors claimed they could hear the teaching sessions a block away. Slowly and painfully this young man (he was 23 when Fred started tutoring him) learned the manual alphabet. He learned the signs for everyday objects, like salt, sugar, pepper, milk, table, and chair. He struggled through a primer with Fred acting out many of the words. Fred would bellow at his student's mistakes. Fortunately, the young man was very deaf and it was the people passing by who jumped when Fred shouted. But six months later this young man could understand many words and would arrive with a smile and sign, "Today—what?" When the lessons were concluded, he did not want to go home. A miracle had occurred: he was learning!

Fred was still very active in the Brooklyn Association of the Deaf. He patiently explained how every club should have both men and women members. He started the first Ladies Auxiliary and Kathleen was elected its first secretary. It succeeded so well that BAD subsequently dropped its sex barrier and opened membership to men and women. Fred's commitment to equal opportunity manifested itself early in his leadership.

One evening a member brought in a new arrival—a deaf man who had escaped from a Nazi prison camp and was living with relatives in Brooklyn. Together, they approached Fred, and the friend of the new immigrant said he would like to make Fred a proposition. If Fred would teach him English, he would teach Fred how to play chess. Fred was a fair chess player already, but the appeal piqued him. Imagine, someone with no money wanting to learn English so badly that he offered lessons in chess! Fred agreed, and the lessons began.

To Fred's amazement, the man was an expert chess player. He patiently pointed out Fred's mistakes and beat him again and again. And Fred taught him English, learning as he taught how complex the language could be, yet all the more determined to help this man establish a basic vocabulary to communicate with hearing people so he could hold a job on his own. With each chess game, the knowledge that *you don't need English to be smart* was driven home to Fred. And with each learning session *but you do need English to communicate* replaced his old philosophy. Thereafter, Fred had a cogent philosophy, one that remained in the back of his mind whenever he fought for the rights of the deaf individual: You don't need English to be smart, but you do need it to communicate with hearing people.

Fred had many friends in the Hebrew Association of the Deaf, and shortly after moving to New York, he joined it. He loved people and admired the smooth-working governing body of this successful group. He often attended the meetings and listened to the debating, occasionally taking part in a heated discussion.

One night he returned from a meeting late at night to awaken Kit with the question, "What would you say if I told you I was elected treasurer of the HAD?"

"I'd say you were crazy," she retorted sleepily.

"Fine," he said, smiling broadly, "I'm not the treasurer, I'm the President!"

Fred, at 28 years of age, became the youngest president of that organization. (He remains the youngest person ever to head it.) His leadership training was accelerating rapidly. Once he had grasped the fact that Ameslan, not English, was essential to social success in the deaf community, he took on more official positions in organizations of deaf people.

On to Washington, D.C.

In 1952, Fred returned to Washington, D.C. The move brought him back to the headquarters of the elite deaf community. Gallaudet College has had a major role in preparing deaf leadership in this century. The college has provided prestigious positions for a handful of deaf college graduates; the federal government also has offered a few opportunities for fairly high-level employment. Many of the college's graduates stayed in the area near it after completing their studies, either winning the few good jobs, or hoping to. Others, like Fred, returned to the Washington, D.C. area after a postgraduate episode in other parts of the country.

Fred's vocation remained in printing for the next 14 years. He shifted after a few years from The Washington Star to the United States Government Printing Office. At the latter he was a compositor until 1966, when he became the full-time Executive Secretary of NAD.

Avocationally, Fred entered into the deaf community's organized social life more vigorously than he had done even in Akron. He joined several social groups in and around the capitol: the District of Columbia Club of the Deaf, District of Columbia Association of the Deaf, the Maryland Association of the Deaf. From 1960 to 1962 he was the editor and founder of the DCCD monthly, *Dee Cee Eyes*. That periodical was an important addition to the Washington scene. It provided a vehicle for shaping attitudes; it was the means of gaining concerted action; it kept the membership informed. The passion for communication—especially in writing— persisted throughout his life. As NAD executive, he inaugurated a monthly newspaper and a newsletter that were distributed nationwide. He felt strongly about involving the adult deaf community in all relevant affairs. The printing press was one way of doing that.

The fourth issue of *Dee Cee Eyes* ran into difficulties. In his editorial in the next issue, he noted:

> That brings us to why you all received your copy of Dee Cee Eyes somewhat late. The Post Office Department had been holding the copies in 'jail' due to a mix up regarding mailing funds, which due to a mistake on their part, they decided we did not have enough money to cover the cost of mailing. We hope that will not happen again, but at least one good thing came out of it all. We were, all of us, gratified to learn how many of our readers actually look forward to getting the paper, and that knowledge should spur us all on to greater efforts in putting out a better paper in the future. (DCE 5/60, 1)

Nearly two decades later, Fred would still be trying to put out "a better paper." He finally succeeded in establishing *The NAD Broadcaster*, NAD's first tabloid, in 1979. But in 1960 he had many other activities to occupy his hours away from his job. The November, 1960 *Dee Cee Eyes* carried a cartoon entitled "Portrait of a Man Who Bit Off More Than He Could Chew." The reference was to Fred, who, in addition to his editorship, was DCCD athletic director and actor-director of a play by the DCCD Drama Guild. Nor did these activities sate his ambitions.

He wanted DCCD to be "the ideal club for the deaf, a club which will serve as a community center for the deaf in this area." Toward that goal, he urged that a literary group be formed within DCCD. Fred's interest in this aspect had a deeply personal side. He read voraciously. Though his tastes were catholic, his favorite leisure-time readings were adventure stories, particularly "Westerns." No Zane Grey novel escaped him. While he read for fun, he saw a serious purpose: reading novels improved his command of colloquial English.

Not hearing speech, Fred substituted reading to keep his English competence at a high level. Being aware of common speech patterns in the novels' dialogues contributed to his superb lipreading ability. Continued exposure to published writing helped his own. The reading habit was one Fred urged on his deaf friends, not by constant admonitions but by his example. In later years, when he travelled frequently, he might forget his razor or a clean shirt, but he was never without books.

DCE gave Fred an opportunity to keep his concerns in front of the deaf community. His Akron experience with orally trained deaf persons led him to review the then-customary educational systems from which they came. In 1962, he addressed his thoughts to the national scene, questioning the composition of a committee convened to advise the Commissioner of Education about deaf education:

The deaf people of this area are advised to keep a sharp eye open for the results of what might come out of the advisory committee for the new Federal Teacher Training program. While we do not mean to get embroiled in the oralism vs. combined method fight at the moment two things stand out sharply in our mind. One is that most, if not all, the deaf who have been taught under both systems are in favor of the combined method and the other is that the deaf as a whole do not express sufficient appreciation for the educators. While we do not mean that we should stop fighting for what we think is the right system in fact we are here advocating that we fight harder than ever, we do think we should stop every once in awhile to give thanks that we have dedicated men and women sufficiently interested in the education of the deaf to fight us. It could just as easily have been that we were left with a situation where nobody cared if we used the combined method, the oral method or any method at all, but we still can't help wondering why the deaf are not consulted more in the matter. After all, we are the ones who are being educated, who were educated under these systems.

We are the ones who are out in this hearing world which we are being taught to get along in and if anyone should know just what value there is to the combined system or the oral system—we should. The orally trained among us presumably use our oral training. The non-orally trained presumably have been struggling along without the benefits of oralism. And the moot question is how are they making out as adult citizens? Can the oralist make himself understood by his boss and co-workers? Can his lipreading stand up under the strain of the non-professional speaking habits of the world around him? And can he go into a restaurant and order a cup of coffee with the reasonable expectation that he will get coffee and not tea? (DCE 8/62, 2)

15

That editorial drew a reply from a federal official, a measure of the column's influence that Fred was certain to have noticed. Mrs. Patria G. Winalski, Consultant on the Deaf in the Office of the Secretary of HEW, responded:

I have read your editorial in the DEE CEE EYES, March 10, 1962, with interest. I would like to reassure you and your members that the question of methodology did not arise among those who supported the legislation which made possible the new Teacher Training Program. Everyone was in complete accord that teachers of the deaf were needed. This same atmosphere prevails among the members of the Advisory Committee which assists the Commissioner of Education in the adminstration of this new law with its recommendations and in receiving the applications for the grants. The deaf are well represented on this committee which includes members who are and have been connected with schools for the deaf, one of whom is deaf himself, and one a parent of a deaf child. Of the other three lay members, two are parents of deaf children and one is a member of the board of a school for the deaf.

I am always delighted to see any group deeply interested in programs and services for the deaf, and I hope your organization will continue its interest and offer suggestions, however, I am a little concerned when I read the issue of methodology being introduced in your editorial. (DCE 8/62, 2)

Over the years Fred had many additional opportunities to exchange views with the writer of that letter to the editor. She remarried, and as staff head of the U.S. Senate's Subcommittee on the Handicapped, Mrs. Patria Forsythe has been a sizeable influence on legislation affecting disabled people. Once he became head of NAD, Fred naturally met her often at hearings of the subcommittee, before which he was called upon to testify as a spokesman for the nation's deaf population.

From his editorial perch, Fred also addressed the entire realm of helping professionals. His words read as well today as they did in 1962:

In July we will witness the first meeting of the NAD since it took on its 'New Look.' This meeting will be one of more than just passing importance since it will be here that the NAD will have to prove that it is an effective organization. And it is to be sincerely hoped that other organizations whose existence has to do with the deaf will be on hand for the proceedings. We are unable to understand how school authorities, rehabilitation people and the like can fail to see the importance of attending these conventions. We would remind the American Conference of Superintendents that the deliberations at Miami will represent the thinking of the products of their schools and their methods of education. If nothing more, it should be worthwhile for them to be there to see just how well they have done as educators. To rehabilitationists—we would suggest they could help people better—do a more effective job—if they knew a little more about the people they are trying to help. We would even hope that oralists will be on hand because there is nothing like knowledge to clear away misunderstanding and apprehension and the amount of ignorance and misunderstanding between the deaf adults and the other organizations which deal with or for the deaf is appalling. (DCE 9/62, 2)

That column also set forth his hopes for NAD. The concerns and the aspirations he expressed preoccupied him for the rest of his life.

Much has been said about the new set-up of the NAD and not all of it has been favorable. Still, we are inclined to think that if the new arrangement is not perfect, it is still an improvement over the conditions of the past. Now, at least, the deliberations of the association will be in the hands of people who are supposed to know something of what is going on. In addition, the people doing the voting will be the elected representatives of the associations for which they will be speaking, which is a far better plan than the old setup where anybody who had the price of a ticket to the site of the convention and a spare dollar or so for dues could vote—regardless of whether he had ever heard of the issue before.

The NAD will be facing some tough problems when it convenes in Miami. One will be the proposal to move the headquarters of the association to Washington. And since we are from Washington we may be prejudiced, but as far as we are concerned this is where the home office should be. The NAD is a national organization. It works on the national level, and this is the seat of the Nation.

Another question is that of NAD participation in the proposed council of organizations. Here, too, is a tough question to settle. The proposal for this council came from the Fort Monroe conference and while it would seem that as written it could stand a great deal of improvement, it is still matter of vast importance to us all. Such a council would relieve the hard pressed State associations from expenses that are common to all organizations of and for the deaf and it is unreasonable for the NAD to insist that it will bear the costs of them all—particularly so since it cannot even bear the costs of the expenses of operations which are exclusively the job of the NAD. (DCE 9/62, 2)

The 1964 Convention

The twenty-seventh NAD convention marked the great turning point in Fred's life. Perhaps "turning point" suggests too sharp a deviation in course. Fred's interest in the welfare of deaf people stretched across his days. His preparation for a leadership role in deaf affairs began early and continued almost without interruption until he attained the executive position he held to his death. So the 1964 convention did not suddenly yield up a leader. It was the time and place when and where Fred attained recognition from the deaf community.

How did Fred see that famous convention? What did he have to say about an event which so dramatically influenced his life? Characteristically, he regarded the actions in proper historical perspective: not as an isolated happening but as the culmination of a series of interrelated events. Equally characteristic is the modesty with which he reported it:

To many, the NAD began a new era in 1964 when the Home Office was moved from Berkeley to Washington. A student of history, however, would disagree with the use of such an arbitrary date or event as the beginning of an era. One would have to go back another four years, to 1960, to understand the developments that led to this move and that are very much a part of the 'new' NAD. In 1960 the State Associations met in Dallas for the first convention under the system of representative government currently in use, a federation of State Associations of the Deaf. This change in the organizational structure of the NAD led to the creation of the District of Columbia Association of the Deaf under the provisions provided in Dallas stating that, for the purpose of the NAD, the District of Columbia should have the status of a State.

The 1964 convention was held in the Shoreham Hotel during one of the hottest weeks of the summer. This convention came hard on the heels of Gallaudet's Centennial celebration and just prior to the unprecedented 1965 World Games for the Deaf, which were also held in Washington. Because the 1964 NAD convention was sandwiched between these two nationally and historically important gatherings, it registered the smallest attendance of any NAD convention in modern times. Nevertheless, the actions taken in 1964 were destined to revolutionize the NAD.

Most significant of the acts of the 1964 meeting was the decision to move the Home Office from Berkeley to Washington, D.C. This motion had originally been made at the 1962 convention, but had been rejected on the grounds that the Association was not ready to accomplish it until personnel were readily available. History should record that the initial proposal came from the Wisconsin Association of the Deaf. (*The NAD Story*, page 12)

Fred does not say that he spurred the creation of the District of Columbia Association of the Deaf. DCAD became his base from which to invade the entrenced NAD hierarchy. *Dee Cee Eyes* gave him the forum from which to rally his supporters. Founding DCAD was also essential to ultimately bringing NAD to Washington, D.C. It would have been incongruous to have the headquarters of a federation of state organizations in a state (as the 1960 convention voted to consider D.C.) without an association.

In 1961, Fred headed a landmark meeting to establish priorities for deafness rehabilitation. Because of its meeting place, the meeting came to be known as the Fort Monroe Conference. The participants set up a clamor for a more active NAD. Specifically, they urged that NAD move from Berkeley, a location distant from the seat of national power, to Washington, D.C. The first attempt, proposed at the Miami convention, in 1962, failed to pass. Fred did not slacken his efforts, and in 1964, the motion passed. Significantly, the maker of the motion, Mr. Robert Horgen, from Wisconsin, had been prominent among those attending the Fort Monroe Conference.

Relocating the NAD headquarters would not have been meaningful without a change in administration. At the 1964 convention, Fred campaigned vigorously for Robert G. Sanderson, of Utah. Sanderson defeated Byron B. Burnes, ending an 18-year reign. As a worthy gesture, the convention extended to Burnes the title President Emeritus.

Fred was elected Secretary-Treasurer by acclamation, a grand salute to the popularity he had won. He took no time to enjoy the honor. He set to work at once to accomplish the move. The convention had designated January, 1965 as the date for relocation. However, Fred pressed for an earlier date, and in October, 1964 the offices opened near the center of the Capitol city, at 2025 Eye Street, Northwest. Without hesitation, Fred took charge of the new offices. He was, however, still a part-time administrator. True, he had been elected to office, but the convention had not yet agreed to the second step in revitalizing NAD—creation of a full-time, paid executive. That step was left to the San Francisco convention.

San Francisco: The Giant Step

With four-year terms assuring their organizational positions, Sanderson and Schreiber focused on gaining acceptance for a motion creating a full-time executive. That goal was not achieved easily.

18

In the December, 1965 DA, Fred presented a description of the head-quarters move from Berkeley into the Eye Street suite. His report filled nearly three printed pages. He detailed the expenses, introduced the personnel, and emphasized the great value of being close to government offices when time came to negotiate grants and contracts. The article was his first in DA and his first as a national officer. His style of writing was immediately evident—candid, exuberant, colloquial—and it remained that way throughout his stewardship. He wanted the members to feel a part of the organization, so he "wrote them into it." He gave a moment-by-moment description of the crises when the bookcases arrived from Berkeley and proved to be too large for the building's elevator or stairs. "Eventually it was decided the bookcases would be sawed in half . . ."

Money was as much a concern of NAD as of any voluntary association. Fred spared the members none of the fiscal anxieties and last-minute reprieves:

> Faced with the unbudgeted and staggering costs of moving, the NAD board considered the feasibility of borrowing to meet expenses, but it was determined that every effort should be made to avoid going into debt if at all possible and the costs of moving and other attendant expenses be met from current income. As a result of this decision, the office remained without additional chairs for several months. Then the NAD secured an evaluation contract from Captioned Films for the Deaf and in order to carry out the terms of said contract it was apparent that we would have to purchase several expensive 16 mm. sound projectors. Here NADer Benjamin "George" Friedwald came to the rescue. Ben provided the name of a Bell and Howell distributor who furnished "demonstrator" projectors at a little over half the list price of the machines. He also volunteered to spearhead a drive for funds to meet the $832.00 that the two projectors would cost. (DA 12/65, 3)

Fred made good use of the opportunity to demonstrate the wisdom of the shift of the home office from West to East Coast. In so doing, he also clearly displayed his own capabilities as an executive. With President Sanderson committed to a year in graduate school, Fred managed the NAD affairs with little assistance. He closed his first DA report with this paragraph:

> Being on the scene we were able to negotiate the Job Corps contract and the Captioned Films contracts. Since other organizations dealing with hearing problems are also located in Washington, we have gone pretty far in mutual cooperation on issues that relate to all of us. And it is entirely conceivable that once we have progressed to the stage where we can have our proposed full-time executive secretary we shall go even further. (DA 12/65, 5)

The new NAD leadership had been working hard for the two years since the Washington, D.C. convention. Finally, in 1966, the full-time position was approved. The convention closed with President Sanderson's announcement of the Executive Committee's choice as first Executive Secretary: Frederick C. Schreiber.

Chapter II
Biography from 1966–1979

F or Frederick C. Schreiber, the second part of his life began with his selection as NAD's Executive Secretary. Once he assumed that office, he and NAD became so closely identified that speaking of one implied the other. Throughout his tenure as chief administrator, Fred had no major interests outside of NAD. It absorbed his days and nights for the seven days of the week. Fred would enjoy hearing that he was NAD's best employment bargain: whatever salary he was paid must be divided by 168, rather than 40, to arrive at his hourly pay.

Such intense effort was essential at first. Every successful organization must have well-developed "M and M"s—money and manpower. In 1966, NAD had neither. What is worse, the prospects for both were fairly bleak. The opening section of Chapter I quotes prominent members' responses to Sanderson's request for their evaluations of NAD. Sanderson, who later became president, was chairman of the Ways and Means Committee when he undertook his survey. It unearthed a picture of NAD as a do-nothing group: Lange called it "just another stand-by organization," Ramger accused it of being insensitive to membership, and Yahn pleaded for evidence to confront those who asked, "Why should we pay that money to NAD?"

Fred fully appreciated the members' discontent. After all, he was a leader in the move to alter the NAD's course. Fred was also aware of two closely related facts: that NAD members were, by and large, impecunious, and that they resented any moves to solicit other groups for what they regarded as charity. As an example of their attitude, the membership undoubtedly supported Burnes when, as NAD president, in 1948, he testified before Congress in opposition to an extra income-tax exemption for deaf people—a concession that Congress granted blind taxpayers.

Fred himself did not fully accept that position, though he empathized with the drive for independence expressed by the decision to reject the

21

extra exemption. In his first report as Secretary-Treasurer, he tells a story which could not help arousing his reader's sympathies:

> The move to Suite 318 was made in June 1965—just in time for the International Games for the Deaf. Numerous visitors were in, particularly from foreign countries, to observe the office—the only one of its kind in the world. It is interesting to note that the NAD was repeatedly urged to take a more active role in the World Federation of the Deaf and while we tried to explain that our organization was unique in still another respect in that it was maintained entirely by the deaf people of America without government grants, the idea was unbelievable. One gentleman from India, a vice president of the India Association of the Deaf, said, 'I cannot believe it—the United States gives billions of dollars to countries all over the world—do you mean to tell me it does not give anything to the deaf of America?' And he repeated—'I cannot believe it.' (DA 12/65, 2)

The deaf leader from a foreign country was astonished by our federal niggardliness. Fred's concluding statement to that anecdote was masterful:

> We were very proud to be able to say that it was nevertheless true and that the deaf of America preferred it that way. (DA 12/65, 2)

In that single phrase, Fred aligned himself with his members. He said what they felt. At the same time, the question posed by the foreign visitor subtly established there was another viewpoint, one held by respectable deaf people, although they were from another country. The outlines of a compromise were only dimly visible. At that writing Fred was a new Secretary-Treasurer and not yet the Executive Secretary.

In reshaping NAD, Fred knew that good works alone would not suffice. An uninformed membership endangers the leaders and itself. Fred began Home Office Notes (HON) within a month after he became Executive Secretary (due to publication lag, the first column did not appear in DA until November, 1966). He missed writing only four columns in the next 152 issues.

HON became Fred's persona. Many NAD members only knew him through his writings. So HON served several functions: advising the members about important events, helping to change their attitudes, and acquainting them with their chief administrator. The columns mix homey detail with announcements of great import—all leavened by a highly personal running commentary. The cumulative effect puts the reader into the executive offices and shreds any mystery about what *they* may be doing there. Candor illuminates every line. Some readers might even feel they are being told too much. Fine, Fred would have said, better that than the complaints that the executive was managing a personal club. The first HON set the style for all that followed. Its opening paragraphs read:

> October was an exceptionally busy month here in the NAD Home Office. The usual business was increased due to the fact that the Executive Secretary had a number of meetings scheduled as well as an increase in the number of visitors.
>
> To bring you all up to date since the last article on the Home Office, we have added shelves in the Executive Secretary's office. These are along two walls and now hold

most of our books and reference materials. More shelves were put up in our 'work-room' and in the storeroom. All are stained redwood and the workroom shelves are arranged so our machines fit under them to conserve space. This adds to the appear-ance of the whole office and while we still are somewhat cramped, appearances are better. (DA 11/66, 4)

Then followed the Executive Secretary's appointments—whom he met, the topics of their discussions—and his travels.

HON aimed to inform. Good news and bad news both appeared. What never appeared were alibis. In reporting about various efforts to get gov-ernment support, Fred noted, "Other VRA applications have to do with the Registry of Interpreters for the Deaf and materials research. The latter has been rejected" (DA 11/66, 4).

Neither did Fred use HON to aggrandize himself. If anything, he downplayed his own role in events, sometimes giving others credit for his leadership or passing off a substantial effort by joking about it. Here are examples of each:

Among the other impacts has been the recent demonstrations by the American Coalition of Citizens with Disabilities. These took place throughout the country in the 10 cities which contain regional HEW offices. One of the demonstrations was in Washington and many members of the Home Office staff took part. Terry O'Rourke, for example, was the local coordinator as a board member of the ACCD. Under Terry's direction we had well over 300 people on hand on April 5 to take part in this demonstration. For the first time it appeared that there were more deaf people on hand than other handicaps, thanks to the Student Body Government of Gallaudet College. Words cannot express the magnificent contributions of the college students in this critical effort. Not only did the students compose a large part of the effort, but the SBG also provided with its own funds transportation for the demonstrators and when it was learned that we were not permitted to send out for food the SBG sent four boxes of peanut butter and jelly sandwiches as well as potato chips and oranges for the starving demonstrators. No matter that the officials at HEW refused to permit them to bring the stuff in, the thought and the effort were most heartening. (DA 4/77, 22)

Nor did his efforts to keep in touch with the membership end with HON. Fred encouraged visitors to the office. He wanted NAD members to concretely experience NAD as *theirs*. In the majority of HON, Fred records visits from distinguished foreigners, prominent government offi-cials, and NAD members. The Home Office staff accustomed itself to working in a goldfish bowl. The openness of the office reinforced the feeling one got from reading the column: nothing was hidden from the membership.

We also had a number of people who just wanted to see the Home Office and wish to remind our readers that we are proud of our operations and welcome visitors. The NAD belongs to the deaf people of America and certainly there is nothing wrong in coming in to see how your office is functioning. (DA 10/68, 34)

Visiting the Home Office was also encouraged by the annual Christmas party, an event Fred initiated his first year and continued for the next dozen Christmases. The party brought NAD members together with influential federal and state legislators and administrators. All enjoyed the open houses—and NAD earned much good will.

Though the burden on him of communicating was heavy, Fred added to it by writing a newsletter:

> In addition to all the other work that was scheduled due to the close of the fiscal year, the Home Office also undertook to get out its bimonthly Newsletter. This was sort of adding the proverbial straw to the camel's back since the workload was well nigh intolerable. However, we have completed this issue and expect that the NAD Advancing Members and the officers of the state association will have their copies by the time you read this. (DA 5/67, 4)

At first it was bimonthly, but later the newsletter went out monthly. Fred's dream was of adding a national newspaper to supplement it and DA. He wanted the newspaper to go to all NAD members. It would carry sports news and articles of transient interest, leaving the weightier, more professional material to DA. Shortly before his death, the dream emerged as *The NAD Broadcaster,* in May, 1979. The newsletter, *Interstate,* continued to go to NAD executives and Advancing Members. And the constant struggle to keep the NAD membership and its supporters informed continued as long as Fred lived.

The Struggles for Financial Strength

The financial condition of NAD in 1966 led the Board to offer to its choice for Executive Secretary an odd arrangement. In effect, the Executive Secretary was told to find his own salary. Fred accepted the charge. It meant taking a fifty percent reduction in earnings initially. He discussed his decision with his wife and children. They accepted the pay cut and gave him the encouragement he had to have. So, in September, 1966, Fred left his assured job in government for the risky position at the NAD headquarters.

His strategy for making NAD financially secure became evident at once. He would put the NAD into business. It would *earn* the money it needed. Fred first had to find sources of revenue other than membership dues. With that he had no difficulty: the federal government had substantial research-and-development programs. Fred approached two federal agencies, and was successful with both.

The U.S. Office of Education had established Captioned Films for the Deaf, in 1959. Fred negotiated a contract to select the films to be captioned. (That contractual relationship continues into 1980.) Aside from the clear logic of having deaf people involved in choosing films to be captioned for deaf audiences, the contract made sense in another way: it paid part of the headquarter's salaries.

The other major "customer" was Vocational Rehabilitation Administration (now called Rehabilitation Services Administration). VRA had funded the Fort Monroe Conference, an effort to set priorities for deafness. As one follow-up activity to the conference, VRA awarded a grant to NAD to teach sign language to hearing adults. There would be a number of other grants from the federal rehabilitation agency, especially grants to establish the Registry of Interpreters for the Deaf and to conduct the National Census of the Deaf Population.

Fred's second task was to convince NAD members that the grants and contracts were not government handouts. The government paid NAD for what it produced. HON made that fact evident. Fred wrote fully about each project, the expenses incurred for it and the efforts made to complete it. The record indicates some challenges were made to Fred's strategy for making NAD financially self-sufficient. Even worse, the influx of money made some members believe their dues were no longer needed.

NAD President Sanderson expressed the dilemma several times in his DA column: members wanted increased benefits from NAD, but they resented paying for them. On the other hand, some members raised specters of governmental interference. Sanderson noted shortly after taking over the presidency that even a small convention registration fee (at that time, two dollars) could arouse severe criticism:

> We had the privilege of reading a sharp attack on the NAD which was published in a southern state association bulletin and republished in a midwest state association paper. Gist of it was that at our convention in Washington, D.C., several misinterpreted incidents were taken to mean that the 'NAD was still out for the almighty dollar.' This was a bit hard for us to take, and was a reflection upon the honor and integrity of the Representatives of Cooperating Member (state) associations attending and upon the NAD administration. (DA 2/65, 27)

A few months later Sanderson felt compelled to respond to attacks by some members who seemingly resented NAD success in obtaining federal contracts for evaluation of Captioned Films for the Deaf. Others apparently believed that obtaining government contracts would prove so lucrative that dues could be eliminated. Sanderson remonstrated at length. Here is a sampling from his editorial:

> I have recently heard two complaints:
> 1. The NAD is 'selling out to Uncle Sam.'
> 2. Now that the NAD has a contract, the states no longer have to support it.
> The first one—the charge of 'selling out'—is ridiculous. The NAD—the officers who are responsible for its administration, and the board members who set policy by their votes, and who in turn were elected by the membership and representatives—will not accept any contract from ANY source (government or private business) that would compromise its principles and ideals. Specifically, the people in government are citizens, just like you and I who have specific jobs to do that were assigned by Congress. They are just as interested in doing a good job for their employer as you and I are for ours. And above all, first and foremost they are loyal to the United States and to those freedoms and privileges which have carried us through perilous years in which despots have enslaved many another country. In short, the people who have asked us to perform certain specific jobs for them are not about to tell us how to do our own work; all we have to do is turn out a product that will meet certain specifications as to quality.

The second complaint is that the states no longer need pay their quotas since the NAD is getting contracts. This is the most insidious and demoralizing argument I have ever heard. It is an expression of defeatism, an admission that the speaker is unwilling to share in the responsibility of management and support of his own organization. (DA 6/65, 29)

Two years later, the same arguments needed to be countered. Fred tried in HON to explain the critical nature of membership support.

We have been disturbed by rumors that some people have the idea that the NAD's government contracts have removed the need for state quotas and state memberships. This is far from the truth. The strength and effectiveness of the NAD rests on its membership base. The more members we have, the more effective we are. And there is plenty of evidence to show that the need for a strong national associaton is as great or greater than it ever was. We are pleased to report that our Advancing Memberships have had a strong upsurge. Latest count gives us 895 individual members. This does not include life members or regular members and is 325 more than we had in July 1966. (DA 4/67, 4)

Of course, deciding grants and contracts are worthwhile does not alone win them. That takes work—and finesse. From the onset of his administration, Fred labored hard, and very rapidly he became sophisticated in dealing with the federal bureaucracy. In 1964, DCAD applied for and received a grant to hold sign language classes for interested hearing adults. Fred asked a friend, Jerome Schein, who was familiar with grant procedures to write the proposal. It was the first of many such joint efforts over the years. Before the first class met, Fred had an atypical bout of pessimism. He bet Schein "the best steak dinner in town" that the project would fail, that fewer than 20 people would attend. Thirty-eight came to that first class. The program was an instant success.

When Fred became Executive Secretary a year later he applied for a grant to sponsor such classes—nationwide. VRA supported the program for the next ten years. Once he grasped the attractiveness of sign language for hearing people as well as those who were deaf, he quickly capitalized on the idea. (Fred was always a fast learner.) The program needed textbooks; NAD published them. The program needed qualified teachers; NAD established the National Consortium of Programs Training Sign Language Instructors (NCPTSLI). Putting the pieces together took time, money, and personnel. Most of all, it needed consistent, visionary leadership. Fred gave it that. (He did not, however, buy Schein the promised steak.)

Fred next negotiated contracts with the Defense Department's Office of Civil Defense and the Labor Department's Job Corps. The former project called for developing programs that would save deaf people in the event of nuclear attack, a possibility less remote in the public mind in the days immediately following the Cuban Missile Crisis than now. The contract earned a substantial sum of money for NAD. The government accepted the report. But interest in Civil Defense has faded and with it any practical results of the project.

26

The Job Corps project carried the Executive Secretary around the country. In camp after camp, he fought the manifest prejudice of managers against accepting deaf recruits. Fred was the best argument opposing such prejudice. The expert on deafness who accompanied him on these travels became his interpreter and Fred demonstrated how effective deaf people can be. Fred led the inspection tours and conducted the inquiries. He won many converts on the road, but distant bureaucrats, not face to face with him, remained resistant to the idea of accepting deaf youth in the Job Corps.

Finding a Home for the Home Office

Within the first year of his tenure, Fred initiated plans for a building. He wanted NAD to own real estate. Equally important was his dream of having all, or almost all, organizations concerned with deafness under one roof. He presented his plan succinctly:

> The Executive Secretary is still looking at potential Home Office structures. A number of buildings have been visited to determine their suitability for our purposes and a few seem to meet our needs. Since the conversion of our invested funds from stock to real estate is a serious step, this is being studied carefully and full information will be made available before any action is taken. The committee that is handling this is composed of Secretary-Treasurer Garretson, the Executive Secretary, Dr. Schein and Dr. David Peikoff with Garretson as chairman. A top price of $55,000 has been set for a building. It is expected that this will not only provide enough space for the Home Office but also space that can be rented to other organizations working with the deaf. (DA, 12/66, 4)

For the next 53 months, Fred dutifully reported the twists and turns, the frustrations of househunting. A brilliant plan for an apartment-office complex is described in the December, 1968 DA, and each month thereafter a no-progress update. Then in February, Fred wrote, "The Home Office building proposal got wrecked." Zoning restrictions. "However, we have been offered an alternate site . . ." So the saga continued. In October, 1969, Fred reported in HON, "As frequently happens, just when we were about to give up hope of acquiring a suitable building to house the rapidly expanding operations of the NAD, we have an offer available which seems ideally suited to our needs and capabilities." He must write in December, "But our building did not materialize . . ." That month NAD headquarters shifted to Silver Spring, Maryland, still into rented quarters.

Once again Fred set down a rationale for purchase of a building. In his New Years greeting, he inserted a theme presented in his first column six years before:

> During the past year we have seen our office staff grow, our spacious quarters taking on a somewhat cramped look as we continually add new projects and new equipment to what we have. The 4000 square feet of space that we felt would be adequate for the next two years isn't. We are so crowded now that we have borrowed space from our neighbors, J.C. Penny's, to keep some of our stock; additional stock including

several thousand books have been stashed away in the home of the Executive Secretary, but these kinds of growing pains are pleasant instead of painful and keeps everyone on his toes. (DA, 12/71, 30)

The May, 1971 DA carried the triumphant statement that the years of search had ended. NAD owned a home. Fred wrote to the members:

By the time this issue comes off the press, we will have completed the purchase of Halex House, which from this day on will be the property of the National Association of the Deaf and the deaf people and their friends in the United States. The purchase of this 21,500 square-foot building marks a significant milestone in the history of the deaf people of America and of the NAD in particular. It is also a fitting start for the 91st year of the NAD's existence even though it is unlikely that we shall be able to take possession of the building before 1972. In the meantime we have our work cut out for us. With first and second trusts totalling $535,000, it is imperative that we start making inroads on this through contributions from our members and our friends. Every administration since the early 60's had been confident that once we have actually acquired our building, deaf Americans would come through as they always have and it is now that this is being put to the test. We hope there will be all kinds of fund-raising activities to insure that we will be able to reduce the second trust as rapidly as possible and that fund raising will continue until we have completely paid off both mortgages. Once the mortgages are paid off, the income from the building will be such as to insure a continued growth in services to the deaf people and an expansion of services such as has never been dreamt of before. Income from Halex House, after the mortgages have been paid off and excluding the space the NAD itself will occupy, will run to about $75,000 per year and will reduce greatly our dependence on grants and government contracts to assure maximum service. (DA, 5/71, 13-14)

Shortly after Fred's death, Albert Pimentel, who succeeded Fred, paid him a tribute he would have relished. Pimentel noted that the purchase of Halex House had proved a great financial boon to NAD:

The NAD Home Office and the varied Halex House operations provide a tremendously supporting and accepting environment for trainees who seldom before had other deaf people like themselves believing that they could succeed in learning and doing many different job tasks. Personally, I feel good walking among these men and women and observing their efforts in building a new independent life for themselves. (DA 9/79, 27)

Fred did not mistake NAD's economic independence as the sole appropriate aim for the organization. The organization existed as a tool for the deaf community to use in achieving its objectives. Without adequate resources, the tool would be weak, ineffectual. Money helped, but getting money was not the target to hit. The dominant culture of the United States respects wealth. Fred knew that, and he sought to bring to NAD the strength that dollars could purchase. He succeeded, and, having succeeded, raised his sights to the next targets.

Writing in the June, 1967 DA, Fred pointed out that the biennial budget called for $79,010. In the June, 1978 DA, he wrote, "We are pleased to announce, however, that for the period 1976–78 our income has exceeded $2 million." The 25-times growth in a decade far outpaced the inflationary rise in that period.

Fred hastened to caution his members: "In noting that the income has increased, we wish also to note that no one should take this to mean that the NAD does not need money and that our fund-raising efforts have ceased" (DA 6/78, 24.) That litany has probably been sung by every executive of a membership group since people first organized. Probably no executive sung it as well as, or more often than, Fred.

By the early seventies, NAD achieved a large degree of financial independence. Increasingly, Fred's priorities shifted more and more to improving services for deaf people and broadening their involvement in national and international affairs—goals which nicely complemented each other.

Publishing

The outpouring of books about deafness which began in the late Sixties obscures the earlier difficulties of getting such material published. The occasional effort by a major publisher met with little financial success. The classic work of Harry Best, *Deafness and the Deaf in the United States,* did not repay the Macmillan Company its publication costs. Experiences like that kept commercial interests at a low ebb.

Soon after becoming Executive Secretary, Fred used his new position to increase the literature on deafness. He did so in two ways: first, by becoming a bookseller and, second, by becoming a publisher. His deep commitment to the written word, his natural sales talents, and his dedication to improving conditions for deaf people encouraged him to undertake what clearly at the time was a gamble.

Fred began modestly with one book, Maxine Boatner's *Dictionary of Idioms.* The book aimed to assist deaf students to master the peculiarities of English, something Fred considered worthwhile (though not as critical as he once had). Also, it had already proved to be popular. In characteristic fashion, Fred's announcement of the new venture was subdued, offered inter alia in HON January, 1968:

> As a matter of fact, the office will grow a little larger a few weeks from now as we acquire an additional 158 square feet of space adjoining our present reception room. Addition of this space will provide us with a 'shipping room' in anticipation of taking over distribution of the American School for the Deaf's *Dictionary of Idioms.*

> This book, which was compiled under the direction of Mrs. Boatner, has met with very wide acceptance and over 10,000 copies have already been distributed to pupils in schools for the deaf. However, the original printing has been exhausted and the ASD has agreed to permit the NAD to take over and thus make the book available to deaf adults also. There is no doubt at all that it is s MUST on every deaf person's bookshelf and we are happy to be able to make it available. While formalities have not been completed as this is being written, it is anticipated that the book will sell for $3.50 a copy and will be available to everyone. (DA 1/68, 31)

The book did fairly well, returning its printing costs, but it did not find a place "on every deaf person's bookshelf." In 1971, Fred took a greater chance, with considerably greater success. He published *They Grow in Silence,* by Eugene Mindel and McCay Vernon. The manuscript had been rejected by its intended publisher, and others showed no desire to publish a defense of a point of view then so unpopular—that deaf children are best taught through a combination of manual and oral communication. NAD, of course, supported that approach, and it distributed the book enthusiastically.

One of the largest financial successes during Fred's stewardship came from publishing *A Basic Course in Manual Communication,* first printed in 1973. The book grew out of an earlier success in what has proved to be a series of important contributions by NAD to sign-language instruction.

Other themes have emerged from NAD's publication list: history, demography, philosophy, etc. Indeed, from 1968 to 1979, NAD published books on a vast range of topics—all in connection with deafness, of course.

To market the books, Fred established a mail-order department in 1967. Modeled after a similar effort begun at Gallaudet College three years earlier, the department first printed up a circular listing books on deafness and related subjects and then mailed it out. It produced a quick, surprisingly large response. Within a short time, mail-order sales of books began to generate significant income. This income created the risk capital with which to publish new books, which in turn generated more income. By 1979, the mail-order department sales reached nearly a million dollars!

Fred took the book business seriously. He attended seminars on publishing, along with Mrs. Barbara Olmert, whom he groomed as manager of the department. Through his studies, he grew in his understanding of the nuances of the book business. His creativity remained undiminished by his sophistication. He wanted, and got, children's literature in sign language and simplified English versions of classics, like *Beouwulf.* All manner of equipment for deaf users—vibrating alarm clocks, kits to change doorbells to light signals, etc.—was added to the book sales. In November, 1969, as he would write many times thereafter, Fred invited readers of HON to the NAD General Store:

> With Christmas just around the corner, readers are reminded that the Home Office has many items which are excellently suited for Christmas presents. Aside from the obvious gift subscription to THE DEAF AMERICAN, we have keychains, ash trays, DEAF AMERICAN binders, the DICTIONARY OF IDIOMS, sign language books . . . all of which make excellent presents and will serve the interests of the NAD as well. (DA 11/69, 33)

"To serve the interests of the NAD," Fred sought some independence from government funding. NAD could *earn* additional freedom. Going into commerce was a means toward that end, a means of getting nongovernmental capital with which to expand NAD's activities. Fred did not dislike federal assistance. However, he wanted to be in a financial position to reject it, if accepting the funds meant accepting external interference in NAD affairs.

Through books, naturally, Fred also sought to educate the general public about the deaf community. He urged libraries to buy sets of books on deafness for their reference shelves. He worked with Lions International on a project to distribute books from the NAD's list. He was especially eager to make NAD's expertise available to parents of deaf children, and so he worked closely with International Association of Parents of the Deaf in developing and distributing literature.

The mail-order business opened jobs for deaf people. Fred would have liked, one day, to have a printing-binding plant of his own. In a small way, he did have one, a very small one, capable of producing short runs economically. But he had much greater ambitions for NAD. Fred continuously melded projects to gain extra benefits from the NAD's efforts. Today the NAD's mail-order operation provides a training ground for young deaf people, with funding from a CETA grant. The mail-order operations exemplify how Fred made one project serve a number of ends:

- earning capital for other investments,
- providing a service to deaf people,
- educating various various groups—the public, parents of deaf children, deaf people, etc., and
- opening job opportunities for deaf workers.

The NAD mail-order department has done all those things. Best of all, it has given NAD members a sense of confidence in their own ability to control their destiny, independently from government aid and imposition.

Other Commercial Ventures

Fred found other ways to initiate enterprises which combined NAD services with capital creation. Making money was never a sufficient objective to justify his attention. Instead, Fred put together goals. He certainly did not regard earning profits as undignified or unworthy of his efforts, but he had the talent for gaining some advantages for his constituents while adding to the NAD treasury. As he had known from the day he became its Executive Secretary, NAD expected its chief officer to earn his keep and not depend upon the dues of its members. The option of taking government handouts never appealed to Fred. He wanted government funding, but not as a charitable contribution. He preferred to work for any federal or state monies, thus avoiding, to some extent, government interference. Having outside sources of income meant greater freedom for NAD—something Fred and NAD's members prized highly.

DEAF, Inc. On a number of occasions Fred said that rehabilitation of deaf people would be better managed by deaf people. Did he mean it?

In early 1977, Mr. Elmer Bartels, head of the Massachusetts Rehabilitation Commission (MRC), invited Dr. Jerome D. Schein, director of New

York University's Deafness Research & Training Center, to open a rehabilitation facility for deaf clients, in Boston. Commissioner Bartels had
become greatly dissatisfied with vocational rehabilitation for deaf clients,
and he wanted a program which could serve the entire state's deaf population. Schein asked for time to consider the proposal and immediately
contacted Fred. They met at lunch in Washington, D.C., with Edward C.
Carney. Fred had been ill and was feeling somewhat weak. His initial
response to Schein was negative; NAD already had enough irons in the
fire. Schein dropped the discussion until the meal was over, then he spoke
magic, for Fred, words: "It won't cost anything!"

MRC would award a contract covering all expenses. Financially, no risk
to NAD would be involved. The Deafness Research & Training Center
would provide the initial management, so no heavy time commitment
from NAD would be required. Carney was enthusiastic. Fred was persuaded, and he agreed to recommend it to the NAD Board for its
approval. He even agreed to the proposed name: DEAF, Inc.—an acro-
nym for Deafness Evaluation and Adjustment Facility. It immediately
characterized the enterprise as being *of, by,* and *for* the deaf community.

Once Fred's reluctance was surmounted, progress came swiftly. Fred
had to convince the president of Massachusetts State Association of the
Deaf, Jack Levesque, to cooperate. Jack was skeptical. MSAD had less
than 50 members and was only three-years-old. However, Jack deeply
respected Fred; they had worked together in the Home Office, where
Jack had been Fred's understudy. So when Fred assured Jack all would
go well, Jack acquiesced. A corporation jointly owned by MSAD and NAD
was founded, and DEAF, Inc. sprung to life in October, 1977. Here is
Fred's first announcement of the venture:

> We are now moving toward the establishment of a new corporation called Deaf Eval-
> uation and Adjustment Facilities, Inc. This new corporation is to be a joint effort of
> the Massachusetts State Association of the Deaf and the NAD. It will own and operate
> an evaluation and adjustment facility in Boston and if successful, will in future years
> as DEAF, Inc., attempt to establish similar facilities in other regions in the United
> States. If all goes well, the new Boston facility will start operating October 1 with the
> Deafness Research and Training Center at NYU providing the initial management
> assistance but eventually the center will be run through the new corporation. (DA 9/
> 77, 43-44)

Jack Levesque rapidly changed from hesitant partner to bold leader. As
DEAF, Inc. took shape, Jack began to appreciate the opportunity it gave
him and the deaf community. He found a most fitting way to express his
gratitude for the bounty put before him. He prepared a magnificent surprise for Fred. Here is how Fred saw it:

> As previously reported, the NAD, in conjunction with the Massachusetts State Asso-
> ciation of the Deaf created a new subsidiary which is called Developmental Evaluation
> and Adjustment Facilities, or DEAF, Inc., for short. On November 20, DEAF, Inc.
> had an open house for its Evaluation and Adjustment Facility located in Allston, a
> suburb of Boston. On hand for the occasion were the NAD's Executive Director and

Dr. and Mrs. Jerome Schein of the Deafness Research and Training Center at NYU, who was one of the prime facilitators for the development of the project. On hand also was Commissioner Elmer Bartels of the Massachusetts Rehabilitation Commission, whose support of consumer-based service organizations had a lot to do with the establishment of the program, as well as many other people in the Massachusetts Rehab Commission, including Peter Tanglos, who is our liaison man, and Frank Sorghmann who located the facility for us and who managed getting the place in shape in time for the ceremony.

But also on hand was Kathleen Schreiber, who was smuggled in to confound her old man and who managed to render him speechless—something which is universally agreed is a most difficult feat. In assisting the Executive Director in unveiling a plaque on the building it turned out the reason for her presence was the Massachusetts people, as well as others involved in the development of the Center, had the notion that it would be a good idea to name the facility the Frederick C. Schreiber Center— and in so doing accomplished the miracle of rendering him speechless the second time in one day, which, as noted, took some doing. Asked to comment on that honor, all we could say is, 'But I ain't even dead yet.' Which is about all one could say under the circumstances. But in the course of the ceremonies, it was mentioned that Jerome D. Schein planted a seed that took root in the soil furnished by the Massachusetts Rehabilitation Commission and watered by the tears that came unbidden from the NAD's Executive Director's eyes, which was about as concise a statement as anyone would care to make. (DA 12/77, 17)

The tribute planned by Jack Levesque proved timely. The Frederick C. Schreiber Center too quickly became a memorial for the eponymous leader.

Deaf Community Analysts. The National Census of the Deaf Population convinced Fred of the dangers to deaf people of faulty research. The NAD-sponsored 1971–72 survey showed that the number of deaf people in the United States, previously estimated to be about 200,000, was only half right: The revised estimate was 410,000! The prevalence rate for deafness used by governmental agencies and others had been based not on careful study, but guesswork. The official rate that had been used up to 1972—1 per 1,000—was invented, not discovered. The 1971–72 survey, by showing that the true rate was closer to 2 per 1,000, exposed the extent of governmental neglect of deaf people. Obviously, if services were predicated on a gross underestimate of the deaf population to be served, then those services fell far below the deaf population's needs. Because the deaf census met rigorous scientific standards, government officials could not brush its findings aside. The results proved an effective tool in Fred's hands.

We also took on some major challenges. Probably the biggest of the efforts was the National Census of the Deaf. For more years than I am willing to admit, people complained about the lack of adequate data on the numbers of deaf people in the United States. It became a sort of joke like what is always said about the weather: 'Everybody talks about it, but nobody does anything.' So we decided to do something and with the able assistance of Dr. Schein the National Census came into being.

One of the more significant benefits of the census was the discovery that there are twice as many deaf people than we were aware of. While there were many other benefits one of the more tangible ones was the realization that the NAD had the capability to handle a task of that magnitude. (DA 2/76, 26)

Still, Fred wanted assurances that future studies of deaf people would be done by thoroughly prepared scientists, adhering to the ethics of their professions. One way to reach that objective was by developing NAD's own organization to do research. Since 1965, NAD had had a Research and Development Committee. The committee had obtained grants for the National Census of the Deaf Population, the study of deaf youth in the Job Corps, and other projects. The committee, however, was made up of persons who could only give it part-time attention. Fred wanted a full-time research organization.

At the Rochester (N.Y.) convention, in 1978, Fred presented a plan to the NAD Board. He proposed the establishment of Deaf Community Analysts, Inc. The Board accepted the idea, and in September, 1978, DCA began operations:

> DCA is a wholly-owned NAD subsidiary and its function is to provide demographic and other kinds of research. It is currently employing another of our former staff members, Marcus Delk, who will be working part-time on that program, and if we have any kind of success, will be at it full-time by the beginning of 1979. Incorporating DCA and getting space set up have been priorities this summer and are now out of the way. (DA 9/78, 37)

DCA began operations with contracts from American Telephone and Telegraph Company (survey to determine deaf persons' TDD preferences), Westinghouse Learning Corporation (a study of the legibility of TV captions), and Public Broadcasting Corporation (survey to determine deaf persons' desire for captioned television.)

The first year's profits were assured from the day DCA began, but more importantly, the research had significant implications for the deaf community. The PBS survey, in particular, led directly to captioned television for deaf viewers.

The Uncompleted Agenda

Fred did not succeed in all he tried, but neither did he fail very often. Mostly, he needed time, more time. From the beginning of his term as Executive Secretary, Fred felt the pressures of too few hours for too much work. He opened two of early HON with almost identical sentences: "October was an exceptionally busy month here in the NAD Home Office" (HON 11/66) and "November was a pretty busy month here in the Home Office" (HON 12/66). He would repeat that statement, with variations, to the end. In HON 5/79, he wrote, "We have found May to be an extremely exciting month," and then he went on to detail an incredible number of issues that required—and got—his attention. Over 14 years, "busy" changed to "exciting"; an attitude change reflecting his experience. His work load grew with his capacity for handling it. He stopped, after a while, measuring his worth to NAD by what was left undone and began to measure it by what he accomplished.

While THE DEAF AMERICAN is getting back on schedule, we are discovering that the Home Office notes take a lot of tending to. For the past two months we have been dwelling on the things we have done over the last decade. We have not mentioned all of the things which we didn't do. Possibly because our readers know them as well as I, and possibly because there are so many that it would take more space than allocated for this column to list them all. But we can at least take note that we know we have not done all that needs to be done and we know, too, that much much more remains to be done. (DA 3/76, 30)

One goal that he set for himself and that he never attained was gaining financial support from The United Fund of America. Fred believed that NAD should receive support for its service programs from the general community and, in turn, participate in the annual fund raising. He first applied in 1966. He reapplied over 10 years, then gave up trying, though he continued to believe NAD deserved better than it got.

Occasionally, time worked in Fred's favor and turned a liability into an asset. Fred did not suppress his pleasure at Dame Fortune's smile, as he reported a happy reversal:

In other areas we continue to move ahead. The CETA program is well under way. At this writing, we have 16 trainees on hand and are somewhat behind because the equipment we will be using has not yet been set up. But we are pleased and proud to note that in the process of setting up this equipment we have resurrected an old machine that has been buried in the office for at least three years. Originally labeled 'Fred's Folly,' this fold/inserter was acquired for the sum of $50.00, delivered to the Home Office for an additional $200.00, and then we were advised that it would cost about $600.00 to put it in good working condition. Spending $600.00 to fix a $50.00 machine does not make sense and so over the ensuing years the machine languished in the dungeon, with the Executive Director resisting any and all suggestions that it be consigned to the scrap heap.

That machine is part of our long range plans and while the plans may be long in ranging, it is in the program. Today the machine is being rejuvenated because the time has come to put it into use, and we are advised that its replacement cost—if we had to buy a machine like that today—would be $20,000. So it is not a bad deal and a good feeling to know that it was not all a wasted effort in both time and money. (DA 2/78, 24)

But Fred was denied what would have been a major triumph—the bringing together of organizations concerned with deafness under one umbrella. Called MAP, for Mutual Alliance Plan, the new organization would do what an earlier one had not done: bring the major deaf groups together to fight for common objectives. Throughout his NAD stewardship, Fred worked to bring together other groups. One of the purposes of Halex House was to provide a physical home for these diverse organizations. Many accepted: International Association of Parents of the Deaf, Teletypewriters for the Deaf, Inc., American Deafness and Rehabilitation Association, National Registry of Interpreters for the Deaf, and International Catholic Deaf Association. However, several major organizations, like the Convention of American Instructors of the Deaf and the

Conference of Executives of American Schools for the Deaf, did not. (Since this was written, they have.)

A significant holdout was the Council of Organizations Serving the Deaf (COSD). Founded as an outgrowth of the Fort Monroe Conference, COSD was to have been the MAP of its day. It did not live up to expectations, and in 1975, it closed permanently, after 9 years. It did not fail altogether. For a time, COSD did bring diverse interests together, holding conferences on important issues. Moreover, it provided Fred with valuable lessons which he hoped to apply to MAP.

Fred saw in COSD the outline for what he believed the deaf community needed. He first writes about "the umbrella organization" in April, 1977. Characteristically, the first mention is modest:

> In other activities we have about completed a draft of the proposed umbrella organization. The draft is now being circulated among the members of the committee that has been given the responsibility of coming up with a workable plan for such an undertaking. Participating in this effort are President Mervin Garretson and Executive Secretary Fred Schreiber for the NAD; IAPD Finance Committee members Joe Geeslin, Bonnie Fairchild, Wilda Owens, Ann Wilson and Mary Ann Locke; TDI members Gordon Allen, Dave Myers and Latham Breunig; PRWAD members Charlie Hill and Rex Purvis. (DA 4/77, 22)

The plan gains a name and a little more explication of its purported role in July, 1977:

> On other fronts we have had meetings that offer considerable promise. The demonstrations staged by the Center for Law and the Deaf regarding the Spellman bill for TTY's has been most effective. We have hopes that a similar bill will be introduced on the Senate side which will be a giant step forward in getting TTY's into greater use. As such and as part of the effort to spread the Mutual Alliance Plan, the Executive Secretary attended briefly the TDI convention in New York. Here he had the opportunity to comment on both the Spellman bill and the MAP and to urge acceptance of both as forward steps in the welfare of the deaf people of the United States. (DA 7/77, 20)

By September, 1977 the MAP takes further shape, and Fred gives it a substantial boost, a prediction that it will be highly beneficial to NAD members:

> And, as previously reported, we will be meeting with a committee from TDI to discuss TDI's possible participation into the Mutual Alliance Plan. It is our hope that the Mutual Alliance Plan will be printed in this issue or in a subsequent issue of THE DEAF AMERICAN so that all of our members will be aware of what we are proposing to do. This project will be as significant and as far reaching as the Fulton Tontine and should have as careful consideration as possible. In future issues we shall attempt to provide a question and answer sort of article to cover the major points of the plan as well as a discussion on why it is being proposed and how it will benefit the deaf community as a whole. (DA 9/77, 43)

Fred next argues that the MAP concept is far from a radical idea. By way of urging its adoption, he sought and uncovered its historical roots:

36

We will also have scheduled another meeting for the Task Force on the Mutual Alliance Plan to see if we cannot devise a better set of bylaws to present to the Convention in 1980. We have made some progress in this, but still have a long way to go. It is interesting to note that the concept of this Mutual Alliance Plan is not new. In fact, it is considerably older than we have been aware. The founders of the NAD recognized the need for a cohesive presentation and made numerous proposals which are being realized only today, so to speak. The current NAD setup was proposed over 50 years ago; the umbrella concept behind the Mutual Alliance Plan also appeared in the early years of NAD history—even at a time when there were but a few national organizations of or for the deaf in existence. It is startling, in a way to realize that recognition of this need appeared so early in the history of the organization, but that it has taken all the years in between to reach the point where the need can be met. (DA 3/79, 35)

He wrote no more about MAP. It remains part of his unfinished agenda.

Personal Finances

One measure of Fred's dedication to and identification with NAD is his willingness to risk his own funds to support it. The financial sacrifice he made in accepting the Executive Secretary's position has already been noted. He did not try to make up for that loss of earnings by supplementing his salary, as well he could. For example, the NAD financial statement for the period May 1 to October 30, 1966 carries the entry "Donation: F.C. Schreiber (Hartford fee) . . . 77.75" (DA 1/67). In view of his low salary at the time, the donation easily can be described as overly generous.

When the NAD building was being purchased, Fred led all members in lending money. He met crisis after fiscal crisis out of his own bank account. He put his personal credit on the line, not blatantly but with quiet determination. Because he gave so freely, he was able to exert great influence on others. His enthusiasm for and confidence in NAD's future infected his friends and acquaintances and converted them to willing partners.

Sickness and Health

The successive illnesses which struck him at age 5 years very likely damaged more than Fred's hearing. Yet he did not slow his pace, did not spare his energy, and invariably joked about his poor health over the years. Even when faced with very dire consequences, Fred did not whimper, nor did he rage. At least for those around him, he appraised the risks openly—and humorously.

In January, 1970, Fred faced the first operation for removal of cataracts. He advised his constituents matter of factly:

The Executive Secretary has been informed that his expected operation for the removal of a cataract in his right eye has been scheduled for January 15. This will mean that he will be out of the office for a six-week period and plans are being made now to take care of his work for this period of time. (DA 11/69, 33)

In May, 1970, he noted his recovery in a single, brisk sentence. "The Executive Secretary is now fully operational with both eyes functioning" (DA 5/70, 33). Such seeming nonchalance must be weighed against the prevailing fear of blindness among deaf people. Already unable to hear, most deaf persons regard loss or impairment of sight with terror. Fred's handling of the threat in 1970 and again in 1975 may not have fooled any who were close to him, but for his readers his behavior certainly was exemplary.

From 1970 on, Fred's eyes gave him some difficulties about which he joked. He would lose an essential corrective lens and remark that he "dropped an eye bone!" Glasses had to be fitted and refitted. More surgery and possible blindness confronted him, yet his smile invariably rushed forward to eradicate any incipient pity from being expressed by those around him.

As chief executive of a national organization, Fred was required to travel. Going about the country can be great fun, but it also exacts a physical toll. Diets are difficult to follow when eating in hotels and attending banquets. Sleeping in strange beds, staying up late and arising early, constant pressure to maintain schedules, anxiety about making connections—these problems quickly disillusion the business traveller. Fred faced them all—and more. Being deaf added difficulties.

Once Fred followed the advice of a friend and advised the airline he was deaf. Airlines have a reputation for accommodating passengers' special needs, such as providing special meals. Fred's special need was for information in transit, the kind of information, like schedule changes, that is usually broadcast on loudspeakers. Airlines announce late departures and gate changes over the airport's loudspeakers, hardly of any use to Fred or other deaf people. His friend argued that, knowing he could not hear such announcements, the airline would seek out Fred and be sure he was kept informed. Also, on the airplane, stewardesses had no other way of knowing Fred was deaf. Even after cataract surgery, Fred's lipreading ability (and his ability to read a situation) often fooled people into believing he heard them. However, he could not lipread the airplane's intercom. In fact, for years Fred was unaware that announcements were made inflight. The revelation occurred on a trip from Washington to Boston, when his travelling companion signed to him that the plane was at 24,000 feet and the temperature outside the cabin was − 10 degrees.

"How do you know that?" Fred challenged.

"The pilot just announced it over the intercom," his companion replied.

Sophisticated as he was and as much travelled, Fred admitted astonishment. "I never thought of that," he said with appreciation for another wonder of his era.

38

On his next trip, Fred accepted his friend's advice to tell the airlines he could not hear. He anticipated stewardesses bringing him inflight information and ground personnel seeking him out to personally inform him about important developments. Instead, when he presented his ticket at the airline counter, he was given a knowing glance. Then, despite his protestations, he was put into a wheelchair and, thoroughly embarassed, pushed to his seat aboard the airplane!

He did enjoy repeating the story for years afterwards as an example of how little the public understands deafness. He did not, however, give another airline advance knowledge about his deafness.

In February, 1973, far more serious illness struck Fred. He suffered a heart attack. It came at a time when he was battling a faction of the NAD Board, led by then-President Don Pettingill, that wanted a greater share of leadership. The personal onslaught became so fierce that Fred considered resignation. Before he could decide, his heart gave way. In characteristic fashion, he announced the damage with humor.

One of the most surprising items to crop up in the Home Office this time has been the fact that the Executive Secretary is not indestructible. As this is being written, the Executive Secretary is presently at home recuperating from a 'mild' heart attack. If we had a choice, we would blame this on the Nixon administration, especially since everything else is being blamed on this administration, so they should not mind one more sin to their already long list of sins. Nevertheless, for timing the heart attack could not have come at a worse time. (DA 4/73, 13)

While Fred was recovering, the NAD Board convened a committee to study the Home Office. In anticipation of the committee's report, Pettingill wrote in the May, 1973 DA, "It is also likely that a complete new organizational structure will be set up in order that one man, the Executive Secretary, will never need or want to run the whole show again."

Expressing no sadness or concern for Fred, Pettingill continued, "The Executive Secretary mentioned at the beginning of his column last month that he was surprised to find (he) was not indestructible after all."

Fred did not reply to these insults—certain not in HON. He focused on the welfare of the organization, kept the members informed of NAD progress and problems, and maintained an outward appearance of good humor. Nonetheless, the assault by the dissidents on the NAD Board wounded him deeply. His personal sacrifices had passed without mention. His successes had earned him only envy, not the appreciation they richly deserved. The jealousies he encountered doubtless delayed his recovery, but he continued to write about NAD affairs, never once in defense of himself. His persistent good humor peeked through, and a year later he quipped to his readers, "Altogether the staffing picture is looking better and it will not be long until our staff is the same size as it was before the Executive Secretary decided having heart attacks was a good way to get a vacation". (DA 7-8/74, 35)

His damaged heart remained very much on Fred's mind. Frequent trips to his physician, painful tests, radically altered diet, heavy medication, the end of his long affair with cigarettes—all these reminded Fred that he now lived under imminent threat of death. Despite that, he barely reduced his work load. A sample of his travel schedule a few months after his return to active duty shows how much more he regarded his duties than his life:

> The Executive Secretary was relatively homebound in September traveling only to South Carolina for a meeting of a planning committee on the training of psychologists to work with the deaf. This meeting is to lead up to a National Conference on this subject in February 1975. The conference being tentatively at least set for Spartansburg, S.C., as a means of making sure there will be no outside distractions and for keeping costs within current per diem allowances. Among the sidelights of that meeting was the discovery that Charleston restaurants were selling Maine lobsters ('three pound Maine Lobster at $19.95') Anybody for sardines? Due to airline strikes getting into and out of Charleston was difficult and the Executive Secretary who was scheduled to speak in Hartford, Conn., on September 21, barely managed to get out of the South and into New England in time. In fact, flying to Hartford proved very difficult and first it was necessary to land in Albany, N.Y. and then change planes and try to get back to Hartford. The Hartford occasion was the 35th anniversary of the Connecticut Association of the Deaf. In addition to speaking at the banquet, the Executive Secretary met with representatives of many of the organizations in Connecticut since, like Massachusetts, it has its own COSD. We tried very hard to explain what the NAD is doing and has been doing and where and how it could function with respect to other organizations. (DA 10/74, 28)

In December he described his journeys from Mexico to Baltimore, with intervening visits to Houston and Baytown, Texas. At each stop he spent hours meeting, meeting, meeting. The health toll mounted. He knew it.

> As this is being written, the Executive Secretary is in the hospital . . . again. This time it is due to two ruptured disks in his spine with the prognosis that he will be out of the office all of June. But we are in good shape. Art Norris—as he has done in the past—will take over the management of the office with the help, when needed, of President Smith. Jerry Schein will represent the NAD at the Social Security hearings in Congress, and we shall have someone working on the bill introduced by Senator Randolph for interpreters for the deaf and readers for the blind in the Civil Service Commission. We also have enlisted the assistance of the American Coalition of Citizens with Disabilities on both bills. One of the main results of this trip to the boneyard is that the Executive Secretary had to cancel a number of speaking engagements in addition to the Congressional hearings. These included the meeting at Richmond's Center on Deafness, the Mental Health symposium in Chicago and the CAID convention in North Carolina. All of these bring to mind the frequently raised question as to why does the Executive Secretary travel so much?

> Briefly stated it could very well be 'He had to.' As indicated above one of the main ways the NAD operates is through the support and assistance from many people— the Art Norrises and Jerry Scheins, the Gene Mindels and Rex Purvises—all of whom can and do come to the assistance of NAD when requested, cheerfully and quickly.

> Conversely, when these same people request the assistance of the Executive Secretary—the same quick and cheerful response is given—must be given—if we are to expect continued support. Another reason is that when a specific invitation is issued, it would be insulting to pass it off to somebody else. We do not wish to indicate by word or deed that anyone is less important than anyone else and in truth all are

equally important and must be treated this way. So the Executive Secretary travels, speaks and participates in countless workshops, advisory boards, etc. Strangely enough this is more work than one expects and people who travel a lot will vouch for this. (DA 6/75, 31)

Fred gave himself little recovery time. In the next three months he journeyed to York, Pennsylvania, then Virginia Beach, Pittsburgh, and Cincinnati. In between trips outside the Capitol area, he spoke to meetings at the University of Maryland, the National Association of Hearing and Speech Action, the National Advisory Council on the Handicapped, and the American Coalition of Citizens with Disabilities.

His regular duties as Executive Secretary—managing staff, juggling finances, responding to mountains of mail, etc.—did not lessen. What is more, he held another full-time position simultaneously, managing the World Congress of the Deaf's first Twentieth Century meeting in the United States! By itself, the work required by that international meeting would have kept an ordinary person busy forty hours per week. Fred was no ordinary person, but the strain on him was unremitting.

In January, 1976 Fred was back in the hospital. Another toll paid, in this instance surgery for a kidney disorder. Within two weeks he was back to work. His travel pace did not slacken; he squeezed television tapings (for PBS's *Nova*) alongside Congressional hearings; his office hours stretched into evenings and ran into weekends.

Fred did not sit back in meetings; he was a vigorous participant. He listened intelligently and commented eloquently on the matters before the group. He kept whatever topic was being considered in view, while mindful of any possible implications for his constituents' long-range interests. He could be warily enthused and cautiously optimistic, but he was invariably ready to inject humor into the discussion and display compassion when appropriate.

Another aspect of Fred's organizational life contributed to the drain on his strength. He did not leave his work at the office. Whether as host or guest, he continued to discuss issues, listen to others' opinions, argue and cajole—into the early morning hours. Groups which invited him to speak frequently "entertained him" long past midnight. Fred regarded these contacts highly. He knew the value of one-to-one conversation to persuade the obstinate, reassure the suspicious, relieve the angered, and soothe the ego-injured. He understood that more decisions are reached over the coffee table than over the conference table.

Fred bought property in Ocean City, Maryland. He kept a boat which he deeply enjoyed. A friend noting his pleasure in skippering his craft presented Fred with a sketch of himself at the helm of his "yacht." (See photograph.). His Ocean City residence always held an overflow crowd of family, friends, and associates. NAD affairs and the pleasures of the sea merged easily in Fred's domicile. Talk leapfrogged from where to get Fred's favorite food—steak—to what NAD should do about housing for elderly deaf citizens.

When he was not absorbed by specific NAD activities, Fred devoted time to other disability groups. He strongly believed that disabled people shared common problems, and should not allow their differences in emphases to prevent their working together. He vigorously supported American Coalition of Citizens with Disabilities. A moment of pure joy— one which must have given him strength to continue for months ahead— enveloped Fred at the White House Conference on Handicapped Individuals, in May, 1977. Suddenly before him, Fred saw the embodiment of a cherished dream. He saw with his own eyes the unreserved sharing of pleasure among deaf, blind, lame people.

> In all of the workshops and State caucuses the proposals put forth by the deaf delegates were enthusiastically and unhesitatingly endorsed. The entertainment at night featured both Bernard Bragg of the National Theatre of the Deaf and the Gallaudet Rock Gospel crew. Both were simply great but the Rock Gospellers literally brought the house down. I was there all three nights and on the final night of the show the singers had people in wheelchairs dancing in the aisles. They were simply unable to quit as the audience deaf, blind, lame, all demanded more, 'More' and in sign language yet. There were problems to be sure, but we are extremely proud of the way the deaf delegates, alternates and observers staged their meetings and strategies to get the message home. (DA 6/77, 27)

In mid-1977 he noted that again his heavy schedule had cost him dearly. Illnesses began to follow each other so rapidly that he could speak of them casually:

> The past few months have been quite hectic. Not only because there was so much going on that the Executive Secretary was in town only long enough to empty his suitcase, but also because we were plagued with illnesses and with major activities that were very time consuming by virtue of their importance. (DA 7-8/77, 20)

At year's end, Fred used mention of his health as a practical example of what federal legislation could mean to NAD members. He was aware of stories about his health circulating in the deaf community. By speaking directly, but humorously, he sought to reassure his supporters, while redirecting their interest to a larger perspective:

> First of all, it seems expedient to report that the record of the Executive Director is intact. For those who are unfamiliar with this particular record, it relates to making an annual trip to the hospital. This has been going on since 1970 and for a while at least it seemed that the streak would be broken because 1977 was unmarred by hospital visits. But on December 6 the Executive Director entered Suburban Hospital in Bethesda to undergo cataract surgery completing a cycle that started in 1970, also for cataract surgery. One of the interesting aspects of this is the comparison of treatment between that first trip and this one.

> The impact of Section 504 regulations on hospitals is clearly evident although it is also evident that hospitals have a long way to go before they will be able to handle deaf patients adequately and with ease. (DA 12/77, 16)

Fred flew off to Iran. He later visited Russia, at that government's request. He hopped from city to city in the United States. He rushed from meeting to meeting near home. The Toll Taker raised the price for these trips.

> The Executive Secretary himself has been banished from the office for a time by his doctor because the old ticker don't tick like it should, but as this is being written, the clockworks are functioning a bit better. Other staff members have been knocked out at one time or another with unusual frequency and when we are not being disrupted by health problems, we have to contend with snow. (DA 3/78, 20)

Coupling information about his deteriorating health with references to local weather conditions did not fool his friends. Rumors increased that Fred could not continue. His trips to the hospital became more frequent. A sober Fred addressed his readers:

> As reported in the April issue of THE DEAF AMERICAN, reports of the retirement of the Executive Director were somewhat premature. Despite the toll taken by our recent illness, I am back on the job and intend to stay there so long as my health and the NAD membership will permit. But I would like to take this opportunity to thank all of the people who sent cards, flowers, fruit and what-not while I was hospitalized. I regret not being able to write to everyone individually but do wish to note that the encouragement from your good wishes not only served to speed my recovery but also provided comfort and encouragement for the members of my family who had become somewhat tired of visiting me in the hospital. Truthfully, knowing that there were so many people rooting for me was a big help and one which contributed measurably toward recuperation. So thank you all again and again for your good wishes. (DA 6/78, 24)

But in May, only days after his release from the hospital, he resumed his travels. He attended a conference at Dulles, flew to St. Paul for a meeting, then to Tucson, and on to Rochester, New York for the biennial NAD convention—his last. Did he realize how dangerous his condition was? Commenting on his travel schedule, he notes that it "was a pretty good beginning for someone just out of the hospital and, according to all reports, just a few feet from death's door" (DA 6/78, 25).

In the fall of 1978 his sufferings increased. His longtime physician made the diagnosis of diabetes. He prescribed daily injections of insulin for a condition Fred later discovered he probably did not have. Fred hated jabbing himself every day with a needle. It hurt. But worse, the insulin lowered his blood sugar, making Fred sick. For almost a year, until other physicians stopped the injections, perhaps Fred daily made himself sick—by dutifully following doctor's orders!

Fred never mentioned his "diabetes" in HON. He did touch on his deteriorating physical condition, with a typically self-mocking slant:

> The Executive Director has gotten into the habit of going to the hopsital when he feels the need to goof off and it must be confessed at this time that we were back in the hospital, this time to get most of our teeth extracted—prior to going to Russia, of course. Fortunately, the operation was a success and only one day was lost from work. But if anybody wants to meet the original Mortimer Snerd, give us a call. If you don't dig Mortimer Snerd, you are either too young or too old to be reading these notes. (DA 10/78, 22)

As 1979 began, Fred seriously weakened. A clear sign—in retrospect—emerged in the introduction to his customary discussion of his itinerary for the previous month: "The Executive Director continues to travel although at times reluctantly" (DA 2/79, 40). How prophetic that phrase, *at times reluctantly,* looks now. Only three words of complaint out of thousands he had written. Next month he wrote:

> At the same time, our normal activities go on. The Public Information Director complains(?) that he has 77 letters requesting information in the Monday mail alone, the Director of the CSP Program is busy lining up programs and places for both the Sign Language Training session and the next National Symposium on Sign Language Research and Teaching. We are preparing a quarterly report for Deaf Community Analysts, Inc. on activities to date and getting ready for a full board meeting of D.E.A.F., Inc., in Boston. At the same time, the Senior Citizens Committee will be meeting in Little Rock, Arkansas, and there is scheduled another meeting of the Centennial Convention Committee as we step up activities in realization that the Convention gets closer and closer and time is running out on us. (DA 3/79, 35)

Normal activities? For Fred, yes. The concluding words of that paragraph's last sentence now appear so ominous. And the following month he began his column with a two-sentence report on yet another warning about his health:

> Since there is no denying the grapevine, let me start this month's column by confirming that it is, indeed, true that the Executive Director did, indeed, black out in Dallas Airport on May 16 and spent that night in a Dallas hospital. Fortunately, nothing was found indicative of the cause of the blackout and it has been business as usual ever since. (DA 5/79, 24)

The blackouts (he had another in Denver a week later) probably resulted from the unnecessary insulin injections. It later was found that other medication he was taking for his heart condition aggravated, rather than helped, him. But these discoveries and an even more serious diagnostic oversight were three months off.

Fred opened his last notes with a guarded comment on his own illness, which he mingled with the unspecified illnesses of other staff members:

> For openers this month, I would like to note that the Home Office staff has been seriously considering recommending that we change the name of Halex House to 'Halex Hospital.' This is because of all the illnesses and injuries that appear to be continually plaguing our staff members ever since the beginning of the year. (Before anyone panics, for the record, I am only trying to be funny.) But it is true that we have had an inordinate share of health problems, not only with the NAD staff, but also with the staff members of other organizations headquartered in Halex House, so that we find ourselves in real difficulty in maintaining schedules. As a result of this, we are not exactly on target but we continue to carry out our responsibilities and, generally speaking, have managed to stay on top of most of our pressing issues although the pressing issues also seem to be more and larger than ever. (DA 6/79, 21)

He wrote as if his members' only concern would be that the NAD business remain on schedule, rather than be concerned about him. Maybe he wrote that way, because it was his own willingness to put his welfare second to the organization's.

In August he came to New York City where he entered the hospital. An immediate change of medication, cessation of insulin, and complete bedrest perked him up somewhat. He had arrived in desperately weakened condition. The new medical team told him candidly that two problems loomed: a severely damaged heart and a large abdominal mass. The latter required surgery as quickly as Fred's general health could permit. The possibility of cancer was not hidden from Fred.

His family gathered at his bedside. Kit, Beverly, and Louis came from Maryland, Bobby from Ohio, and Beth from California. On August 31 Fred went into surgery. Characteristically, he demanded that the nurses show him the "Scars Book". He wanted to select the style scar he would have postoperatively. No doubt he made other jokes before succumbing to the anesthetic, but surgical staffs do not record such transactions.

His surgeon did recount later that for 30 minutes he delayed the operation in order to obtain expert cardiological consultation. He found Fred's heart so damaged ("He practically had only half a heart") that surgery seemed too great a risk. The medical consultants, after reviewing all the evidence, concluded surgery must proceed, because the threat from the suspicious abdominal mass was too great to justify further delay.

By late afternoon the verdict arrived: success! The abdominal mass consisted of gall stones the size of golf balls. No cancer. Fred had been afflicted for years, judging from the stones' size, by a diseased gall bladder. Many of his earlier sicknesses could now be explained: misdiagnosed diabetes, inappropriate medication, and completely overlooked gall stones. The future looked very bright. Except for Fred's heart.

Through September 5, Fred remained in the intensive-care unit. He did not have sufficient strength to communicate readily. Only his wife could understand his manual mumbling. The tubes in his nose and mouth made his speech equally indistinct. Throughout his hospitalization a family member or interpreter was with him constantly. In the intensive-care unit one nurse who attended him was thrilled to be serving the man who published the sign book she was studying. She had little opportunity to try her newly learned signs with him. He was too weakened, and others more expert than she at manual communication were always nearby. Fred's physicians also remained on constant alert.

Wednesday, September 5, Fred began to rally. He seemed to be regaining strength. His physicians made arrangements for his transfer the next day to a regular room. His sons left for their homes; his daughters also planned to leave. Conversations with the family centered on how Fred should be managed medically, after returning to his home in Kensington. The optimism of all those around him seemed to touch Fred. Suddenly, about 5:30 p.m. his heart collapsed. His wife and daughters and two friends were with him as heroic efforts by the medical team kept Fred alive until 11:00 p.m.

Then, openly crying, his surgeon came into the waiting room and announced that Fred had died.

The Centennial Celebration

On August 25, 1880, in Cincinnati, Ohio, a small group of deaf men held the First National Convention of Deaf-Mutes. The convention proclaimed, "We have interests peculiar to ourselves which can be taken care of by ourselves."

Three thousand deaf adults and their supporters reconvened in Cincinnati, the week of June 29, 1980, to celebrate the hundredth anniversary of NAD. The events included an extensive array of meetings and workshops, covering a broad spectrum of issues of interest to deaf people. Over 80 exhibitors paid nearly $20,000 in fees to present their products and services to the convention visitors. An original play by and about deaf persons was performed. Miss Deaf America was chosen. Prominent deaf persons and professionals who served the deaf community received awards. The ceremonies were punctuated by visits from prominent government officials. Every aspect of the convention attested to NAD's solidity, its widespread influence. At 100 years of age, NAD had grown large and vigorous.

Fred had looked forward to the Centennial Convention. Plans for it began at the Rochester Convention two years earlier. In December, 1978, Fred characterized his hopes for it:

> At this time we have a very ambitious program set up for the future . . . The Centennial Convention Committee has great plans, and is making huge strides towards insuring that the Centennial will be something that will be remembered for the next one hundred years. (DA 12/78, 41)

Fred had predicted a record-smashing attendance of 5,000, offering to do a striptease, if that number was not reached. He was spared the embarrassment.

The attendance was highly satisfactory evidence of NAD's strength. Equally evident was the participation of many national organizations. The National Registry of Interpreters for the Deaf gave its interpreting services as a birthday gift. The Deafness Research Foundation and the NAD used the occasion to give three awards of distinction, two in Fred's honor. American Deafness and Rehabilitation Association held its national meeting in Cincinnati so that its members could also participate in the centennial observance. International Association of Parents of the Deaf, a particular favorite of Fred, also coordinated its convention with the NAD celebration. These voluntary organizations joined with a dozen or more foreign governments—Russia, Bulgaria, France, England, to name a

46

few—which sent representatives to wish NAD a "Happy Hundred." Fred had visited most of them in their own countries. Now they had come to pay him a return compliment, posthumously.

The Junior NAD also held its convention concurrently with the NAD Centennial Convention. Fred had long advocated more active participation by young deaf people in the NAD. Thanks to his persistent advocacy, Junior NAD delegates had full voting rights at the business meetings and broad participation in the parent association's activities.

As Fred would have insisted it should be, his absence from Cincinnati did not dull the proceedings for most who attended. The Centennial Convention provided a memorial to his great work. Had he been there, Fred would have put in hours of tiring labor, smoothing ruffled feathers, correcting oversights, meeting emergencies. The crowd would have given him no rest. And he would have relished every minute.

The two thousand persons attending the Centennial luncheon bowed their heads for a moment of silent prayer for Fred. Then the affair moved on to other NAD business.

Ave Vale

While awaiting surgery—surgery, he had been warned, that would be dangerous—Fred noted the impending deadline for HON. Rather than miss a deadline, he wrote these last notes on a lined tablet, planning to finish them later. Perhaps he hoped to add word of his successful surgery. In any event, his last HON is much like his first: informative, future-oriented, and ambitious for deaf people. He inserted mention of his own health as a passing comment.

By now I guess people have decided that we have abandoned *The Deaf American* for *The Broadcaster*. But as you can see, the DA is very much alive, and we intend that it shall remain so. In the meantime, we continue to seek correspondents for *The Broadcaster*. So if you are interested in writing local news, there is still time to send in your copy. Subscriptions to *The Broadcaster* are selling like hot cakes. We have established a single expiration date—September. People who subscribe in mid-year will get back issues, but there will be no pro-rated payments and one common expiration date.

One thought is to offer both the *DA* and The *Broadcaster* for a combined subscription rate. If this appeals to you, contact your regional Board Member and let him or her know.

We are pleased to announce the appointment of Albert T. Pimentel as NAD consultant. Al will work part time until January 1980 when it is expected he will become the full time Assistant Executive Director for National Affairs. In this capacity he will represent the NAD at the Federal Administrative level. He will work with our legislative counsel, Jack Duncan, and the Executive Director in developing legislative proposals for congressional consideration and the Assistant Executive Director for State Affairs in exploring Federal funding for State Associations. In addition, he will be office manager and in charge of the Home Office in the absence of the Executive Director.

The Executive Director, incidentally, has been at it again. Suffering an attack of phlebitis in early July, he spent 18 days hospitalized; then 21 days in convalescence and as this is being written, is in New York University Hospital preparing for surgery.

Nevertheless, we are moving along well. Elsewhere in this issue is up-to-date information on the Centennial Convention. We are informed that one of the featured shows, 'Tales from a Clubhouse', which is an original play from Bernard Bragg's Model Community Theater for the Deaf, is well under way. President Emeritus Byron Benton Burnes has completed the Centennial history of the NAD, and it is being edited now. We have also completed our formal application to establish a national credit union and are preparing brochures describing how you can join and the benefits and guarantees the credit union covers. Credit union participation will mean an additional role for State Associations as each Association will need to establish a credit committee to recommend applicants. It is a 'members only' deal which we hope will increase membership as well. At the same time, we welcomed back the Registry of Interpreters for the Deaf. The RID moved back to Halex House in mid-August, ably assisted by Joe and Joy Heil. Joy, you may remember, was the secretary of the Executive Director of both the NAD and COSD and official NAD interpreter on the World Federation of the Deaf tour to Varna, Bulgaria.

He wrote no more. These last words are not complete, only half enough for HON. Fred must have expected to finish the column after surgery. In the meantime, he used his last strength to draft one more message about the future—to plant one more rose for tomorrow.

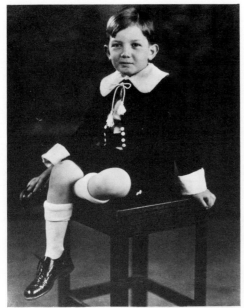

Little Lord Fauntleroy, age 5

September 23, 1944

"Still new executive" pose in the first N.A.D. home office in Washington, D.C.

Fred presenting gavel to new N.A.D. president, Robert G. Sanderson, 1968

*Gallaudet College President Edward C. Merrill, Jr. applauds as Professor Leon
Auerbach congratulates Fred. Doctoral hood was placed by Dr. Wilson Grabill*

Citation

of

FREDERICK C. SCHREIBER

on being presented the degree of

Doctor of Laws, *Honoris Causa*

Gallaudet College strives to offer a challenging academic
program for deaf people: preparation for a full life in a changing
world. It is not easy. It cannot be. Life for a deaf person is not
easy. Yet, with the proper intellectual tools and commitment to
purpose, it is possible for a deaf person to emerge as a national
and international leader.

Frederick C. Schreiber, of the Gallaudet College Class of 1942,
has served as executive director of the National Association of
the Deaf for over ten years. During this time, he has contributed substantially to molding the NAD into an effective
structure, establishing its status as a national organization,
extending its programs and services to deaf persons across the
nation, and shaping it into the primary advocacy group for and of
deaf people in the United States. As project director of the
Congress of the World Federation of the Deaf in 1975, his
organizational ability and drive resulted in the most productive
international meeting which has been held by that or any other
group.

Gallaudet College is pleased to recognize Frederick C.
Schreiber. He went among his deaf colleagues and there found
vast ability, talent and at the same time, frustration. He gave
them purpose and structure through which to work; thus, he
contributed significantly to the creation of the effective deaf
American citizen. In so doing this, he inspires others to try their
hands at miracles.

GALLAUDET COLLEGE
MAY 23, 1977

Faking it in Las Vegas

Seated, l to r: Granddaughters Toni and Stacey, wife Kit, Fred; Standing, l to r: Granddaughter Terri, son Buddy, daughter Beth, son Bobby, daughter Bev and son-in-law, Jimmy Perrell

Co-founder and charter member of the world's first Lions Club Of Deaf Men, Fred poses with club members and visiting dignitaries

Filming a TV program on deafness

Rare moment of relaxation with Kit and Blondie

Fred being hugged by Nanette Fabray despite having sung "Let Me Call You Sweetheart" decidedly off-key

Vice President Fred pays close attention to the speaker at a meeting of the Board of Directors of the World Federation of the Deaf

With Chaim Apter at the Helen Keller Home in Israel

One great leader greets another

Captain Fred at the helm of the good ship N.A.D. as depicted by artist Ruth-pete

Chapter III
Selected Papers of Frederick C. Schreiber

How many published articles were authored by Frederick C. Schreiber? The answer remains vague. Fred did not spend time on a vanity list. He wrote to communicate with his contemporaries. Something at the moment moved him to write, to express an opinion, to refute an argument, to urge an action. In his earthy, logical way, he might ask, "Why bother?" Who would care about volume numbers and dates? He wrote not to bolster his ego but to advance a cause. He seldom looked back. For those reasons, he speaks eloquently to the future.

Herewith, a sampling from his articles and published speeches. The preceding quotations from HON have familiarized the reader with Fred's style. Only minimal editing has been done on the articles that appear next, editing mostly to conform to a single style or to clarify a point obscured because the article is removed from context. Otherwise, what follows is authentic, inimitable Fred.

Recruitment of Interpreters By and For the Deaf

Speech delivered at Workshop on Interpreting for the Deaf, Ball State Teachers College, 14-17 June 1964.

The question of recruitment of interpreters for the deaf is a complex one. It is generally considered today that we have no program in connection with this vital aspect of deafness and, because of this, speaking of recruitment is something like trying to put a roof on a house before the walls have been built.

But it is wrong to assume that we have no program. At present we have at least four minimum requirements with regard to interpreters. These are: they must be able to hear; they must be able to sign; they must be willing; and they must be available. It is about the absolute minimum. It is doubtful if you could get any lower standards than that. Even so, we find glaring lack not only of available interpreters as such but an even more distressing lack of knowledge on the part of the deaf as to who to see and how to go about securing interpreting services when they are needed. It has been assumed that interpreters are usually more readily available in cities and other heavily populated areas and, conversely, are lacking in the rural sections of the country. But is that right? I doubt it. For one thing, in the cities, deafness is an impersonal thing. The average city dweller expects that the deaf man either has three heads or something similarly startling, and as a consequence, when the need for communication with a deaf individual arises, he does not know how to go about it, and all too often the deaf person is unaware of where or how he could secure help in this line, even though he has seen interpreters used before. It just doesn't occur to him that they could also be used in personal matters as well as before groups.

On the other hand, the deaf in rural areas, having lived in a small community all their lives, are well known, their difficulties are known to their neighbors and as a result while there may not be many available interpreters in these locations neighbors are there on many occasions in which they are needed.

Presently, we have two basic sources on which we draw for interpreting when needed. These are our children and the educators of the deaf who are familiar with the sign language. Neither of the two, however, has a full concept of the function of an interpreter and, as a consequence, the full value and benefit of a competent interpreter is yet to be appreciated. In addition, the demand on the schools for interpreting services has grown to alarming proportions. While it is realized that the school people are truly interested and have made great sacrifices to be of service, there is such a thing as beating a willing horse to death, and that is not too far in the offing in this case, since nothing has been done to alleviate the situation or to seek new interpreters to help carry the load. It must be remembered, also, that in most cases, interpreting is done voluntarily, and there is and never has been much percentage in looking a gift horse in the mouth. So long as the services of interpreters are obtained on a voluntary basis, there is little hope for the establishment of standards of competency that must be made before we can hope to get away from the minimum levels on which we now rest, and little hope for the creation of an effective recruitment program unless such standards are set.

An effective recruitment program must of a necessity have several prerequisites. We must be prepared, before we can hope to effectively induce people to take part in this program, to list accurately what we need interpreters for. The need is not and should not be limited solely to the courts. Nor is it enough to throw in meetings, after-dinner speeches and commencement addresses and call it a day. Some effort must be made to assess the fields in which they will be used. Then we have to set the standards of competency that will be required of them. It is obvious that the mere ability to hear and use signs is not enough. On the other hand, we could set a very demanding program, one in which a recruit would have to spend considerable time and effort in mastering all that is required of him. In such a case I would suppose people would think twice before volunteering for any arduous program of training. And finally there arises the question of compensation. Who will pay for these services? This is one of the biggest stumbling blocks in our path. There are some people who feel that the deaf themselves should pay. There are others who believe that the community should pay, and whatever results, the fact remains that to get effective service, reliable service, the compensation must be adequate for the job. Without this, no recruitment program could be successful.

Once such prerequisites are settled, and assuming they can be settled to the satisfaction of everyone, then what? Who will do the actual recruitment, and how? The relation between an interpreter and the person for whom he is interpreting can be a very personal thing. As such, it would never do to just assign any one who happens to be handy to the task. Some kinds of interpreting require special knowledge; some situations are so personal that any success will depend largely on the compatibility of the interpreter with the person for whom he is interpreting; some situations will be such that only a woman could serve as an interpreter and still others will be a "men only" deal. And in still other cases, the personal relationship between the deaf person and his interpreter will make a great deal of difference. There are undoubtedly times when the choice of the interpreter should be left to the client. There are also times when not only an interpreter, but also another deaf person will be needed to translate what is being said into language that both the client and the interpreter can understand. Thus it seems obvious that insofar as is practical, we must consider recruiting panels of interpreters—men, women, and literate deaf people of both sexes to meet these situations.

We must remember also that the sign language like any other language varies from region to region, and to attempt to force it into a standardized form would be like trying to dam the stream of life—a pebble at a time. That being the case, who should handle this project? Recruitment itself, must of a necessity be on a local basis, but what of the other aspects?

It may be possible that the National Association of the Deaf and its cooperating State associations can provide the initial impetus to a recruitment program. It might also be helpful if all the other national organizations of and for the deaf could lend a hand, at least in the beginning, to disseminate the information, to make available to as many people as possible, the existence of such a recruitment program and the requirements and compensations that go with it. By putting the program under the direction of a national organization of the deaf, we can at least insure that the standards and methods of determining compliance to these standards will be uniform, even if the signs will not. It will or should also insure that an up-to-date list of eligible interpreters in all parts of the country would be available when needed, no matter what the purpose.

There is a great need for personnel in this field. One could easily say that under ideal conditions, we would have registers of interpreters in the offices of almost every public and semi-public agency: judicial, police, medical, educational, social welfare, rehabilitation and religious organizations. All these groups could use such information as to where and how to secure the services of interpreters when one is needed. And it must be remembered that the need for interpreters works both ways. We can have deaf people who are confident that they speak with astounding clarity who are actually incomprehensible to the people with whom they are trying to communicate. We can have others who will try to communicate via pencil and still be incomprehensible to those with whom they are trying to talk, and these hearing people might have to, or at least wish to, call in an interpreter in self-defense.

When all is said and done, the actual recruitment of interpreters seems to depend on the kind of program that can be devised here. Given a reasonable program which defines the fields that interpretation will cover, the standards of competency that will be required of the recruit, and an adequate fee system to make the effort of meeting these standards and the inconvenience and expenditure of time worthwhile, recruitment can take care of itself.

The inclusion of organizations for the deaf as well as of the deaf could serve many purposes. For one thing, there are the requirements of the orally deaf. For my part, they need interpreters as much as anyone else, but I would not presume to suggest how we might meet this need. For another, there are several sources of potential supply which might become available to us once a formal program has been established. Social workers and rehabilitation field agents, for example.

Just how far we could go in the recruitment of interpreters seems to depend mainly on the program that is devised. The number and function of interpreters, within the broad range of a national program, would probably be a matter for local determination, since situations will vary from community to community, depending on not only circumstances, but also the extent of services each community will attempt to provide. A program geared to meet the needs of only the courts would naturally require less interpreting than one that attempts to provide all-out community services.

I have said enough, I think, to make it plain that I believe that recruitment will depend mainly on the sort of a program that you devise. Given a practical, workable plan, so arranged that the deaf people for whom it is intended will use it, we can find an ample number of recruits for all our needs. Failing that, we can always fall back to our minimum requirements.

I have said more than enough. I think the rest is up to you. Thank you.

The Deaf Adult's Point of View

Presented at the Teacher Institute, Maryland School for the Deaf, Frederick, Maryland, October 17, 1969

When Dr. Denton invited me to speak to you this afternoon, I felt like a seven-year old turned loose in a candy store. And like a seven-year old I soon discovered that with so many goodies available I was having difficulty in choosing a place to start and if I sampled them all I was in danger of getting a verbal tummy ache.

So I decided to stick to what I know best—the deaf adult's point of view. We find education of the deaf is a complex thing. There are times when we wonder if anyone knows what he is doing in this area. Our first question is—Education for what?

It frequently seems to us that the parents in particular are concerned with education for education's sake rather than what it is supped to do for their children. Last Friday Dr. Ray L. Jones, of San Fernando Valley State College, in speaking on mental health problems of the deaf in Texas, quoted a poem which he said was typical of our approach to mental health and which, in my opinion, applies as well to education of the deaf. Unfortunately, I did not copy the poem but the gist of it had to do with the problems of the people who lived in a town adjacent a steep cliff.

Because they lived near a cliff, people were continually falling over it; and, faced with the decision of whether it would be better to build a fence by the cliff or place an ambulance down in the valley, the town decided to place an ambulance in the valley. Well, people still fell off the cliff, but the ambulance was there in the valley to cart them off promptly. When it was suggested that perhaps a fence on the cliff would be better, the response was Why? The ambulance down in the valley is giving adequate service. We may not be preventing our children from falling over educational cliffs but we certainly have the best ambulance service in the world. [Editor's note: See page 69.]

We think parents of deaf children are the most dedicated, self-sacrificing and short-sighted people we know. This is because there has been so little contact with the adult deaf. While there is no doubt that education is a tremendously important issue, the fact remains that your child will be concerned with education for but one-third of his life. What about the remaining two-thirds?

There are many problems facing the adult deaf today. These problems, unless they are taken care of, will be inherited by your children tomorrow. These problems vary widely, covering needs ranging from legal rights to socio-economic factors and it is a fact that the deaf do not have the kind of people within their own ranks to cope with these problems. There are no deaf doctors, lawyers, public relations men or the like. However, since deafness is no respecter of persons, all these professions can be found among the parents, who can, if they will, do wonders in easing the pressures their children must eventually face. To do this, one must know what the problems are and to know the problems, one must know us.

I do not want to discuss these problems now, but would love to take them up later if time and interest permits.

To get back to education—last year a superintendent of a midwestern school for the deaf wrote an article entitled, "Deaf Education—An Educational Miracle." In this article the Superintendent defends the low achievement of deaf school leavers as being an educational miracle and contended that to expect more from education was asking too much. The funny thing is—I agree with him, insofar as the topic goes. It is truly a miracle that the deaf get any education at all—but not for his reasons.

When a deaf child is born, his parents are advised to toss him into the sea of knowledge and let him sink or swim. The parents are told at the onset that because of his handicap he is the equivalent of a one-armed swimmer, so it is likely that the swimming lesson will be hard. They are further advised that since the child must eventually compete with swimmers with two arms, it would be necessary to hang a 100-pound weight around his neck, also, so that, if he doesn't drown, then his one arm will be twice as strong and therefore capable of doing the work of two.

This is the true miracle. It is a tribute to the deaf that they survive at all under such conditions. Lesser people would have gone under at the outset and most would have given up before long.

Recently a report on the use of Cued Speech referred to it as a crutch and implied that the use of such a crutch would be detrimental to the child. But what's wrong with crutches? The on-legged man used them to take his rightful place in society. He is not compelled to make his one leg serve unassisted in place of two. The blind are not required to see with their ears. Why must the deaf be compelled to hear with our eyes?

You have been told that if your children are permitted to use manual communicaton they will not try to talk, and sometimes this has been demonstrated to be true. This is ridiculous! Deaf children are human and they can see that the majority of the other children talk, so they have to try. Every parent has been exposed, at one time or another to a child's plaintive, "But mama, *everybody* does it." And for those who do not talk—Well, I have a story which may cast some light on the reasons.

When I was seventeen, I had a bad case of hives. As a result, my doctor put me on a diet for two weeks. This diet consisted solely of tea, toast, canned peaches and lamb chops. To make matters worse, at the time I was working as a bookkeeper in a restaurant, and it was real agony to stick to such a diet. At any rate the two weeks finally passed and on the 15th day I came home for lunch which was—you guessed it—lamb chops. I stormed out of the house ignoring my bewildered mother's plaintive, "I don't understand—you always liked lamb chops!" And I have never eaten lamb chops since.

Deaf children have had a steady diet of talk, talk, talk for 9 or more years, whether they could or not. If 15 days of lamb chops could do this to me, 9 years of an enforced diet of speech could do worse. We'd like to know, too, why the insistence on speech anyway? What is in it that makes one think it is the endall of deaf education? Parrots can be taught to speak, so can mynah birds, but no one gets excited about that. Somewhere I read a short poem about a Deaf Child's Prayer. I have not found it again, but the last two lines went something like this:

. . . . . the only words he knew,
"a ball, a fish, a top, a shoe."

It was a cute poem no doubt, and I am sure many people were touched by it, but it filled me with rage to think that a child could have lived so long with a vocabulary of only four words—"a ball, a fish, a top, a shoe."

We are told we have to live in a hearing world and hence must talk. What's a *hearing world,* anyway? The deaf adult, whether he can speak or not, works with hearing people. He goes to the same doctors, patronizes the same stores as people who can hear and, depending on his ability to communicate, he has the same successes as his hearing peers. If living in a hearing world means social living, then ask some of these people who advocate "integration" when did they last have deaf people over to their house for cocktails or a dinner party. Even those of us who have excellent speech and better-than-average lipreading skills are rarely if ever asked.

I do not want to give the impression that I am against speech or lipreading. If I were, I would not be talking to you now. We all know that to be able to speak and read lips is desirable and should be sought after. We believe that every child should have the opportunity to learn to speak and read lips, just as we believe every child should have the opportunity to be another Van Gogh, or Beethoven, or Edison. But our first need is to be able to communicate.

Communication is not speech! You might say that is is not even language. You can communicate a lot with a wink, a hug, or a pat on the shoulder. You can express more displeasure with an angry shake of the head than with a two-hour lecture.

Neither is speech language. Speech helps convey language, of course. It is useful in communicating, also. But one can have speech without language, and one can communicate without either.

I see we have with us today Dr. McCay Vernon. Dr. Vernon is one of the people who has demonstrated a real understanding of the deaf. He has written many articles and offered many suggestions to parents as to how they can effectively cope with their problems. Invariably, he has suggested that parents get to know the adult deaf, to subscribe to our magazine the *Deaf American* and to learn as much as they can about the conditions under which we live. One thing I don't believe he mentioned, however, is what might be the basic reason for becoming involved with deaf adults: we are your children grown.

We can, in many instances, tell you the things your child would like to tell you, if he had the vocabulary and the experience to put his feelings and needs into words. We, too, had parents who went through all the anguish and indecision you face. We have experienced all the bewilderment, all the longing your child has now and some of us, if not all of us, can put these needs and wants into words. If I were your child, I would want to tell you my greatest need is to be able to communicate.

I need more than anything to be able to understand you and to make you understand me. I need to be able to sit with you and ask you why? To ask you to help me explore the universe around me. To understand the do's and don'ts of everyday living. These are hard things to learn; don't make them any harder for me than they already are. Give me the freedom to ask and understand in the easiest way possible—if there is an easy way.

Talk to me, yes, but give me the help that I get from signs and fingerspelling. Remember, I don't speak nor lip read too well.

I want all members of my family, my father, my mother, my brothers and sisters to be able to communicate with me. I don't want to be a guest in my own house. I need to feel that I belong to you and you belong to me as well.

If you will use the simultaneous method, then use it all the time in the home. Aside from the fluency that it will give you from constant usage, I need to be able to *oversee* what my brothers and sisters normally *overhear*. I need the constant exposure to language that this can give. I need to know how third-person conversations are handled. I also need to be able to see for myself what happens to me within the family does not happen just to me—nor just because I am deaf.

Communication is my greatest need. Given adequate means of free and easy communication, I can acquire language and possibly speech as well. I will also acquire the things I need to know that are not formally taught in school and that will help me to grow up to be a well-adjusted citizen, able to handle the demands of the world around me.

I need to know, too, that you don't blame me for all the trouble I am causing you and that you aren't ashamed of me.

And I must say, as Executive Secretary of the National Association of the Deaf, that parents have every reason in the world to be proud of their deaf children. The NAD is the oldest national organization of the deaf in this country. 1980 will mark its first 100 years. Today the name is somewhat misleading since, while it is called an association *of* the deaf rather than *for* the deaf, many of our members are people who can hear; parents, teachers, vocational rehabilitation counselors, among others. But since the administration of the association is in the keeping of deaf adults, the name has been retained. As an association, we try to better conditions for our members and future members: better educational opportunities and facilities, more employment, and the removal of discriminatory practices that exist as bars to employment. We help recruit personnel for professional training in areas relating to the deaf and serve as an information-and-referral center. Among the projects in which we are currently engaged are the National Census of Deaf People, a project which we expect to complete in 1972. We also have a Communicative Skills Program which conducts classes in signs all over the nation. In addition we have the Registry of Interpreters for the Deaf, all supported by federal grants. We have contracts for such things as evaluating general interest films for the Captioned Films program, and we have inhouse projects, such as the Junior National Association of the Deaf, which is a school program designed to make our youth more aware of the responsibilities of citizenship and to develop leaders. Daily our office receives letters requesting information or asking for help with problems which cannot be taken care of by independent action. It is from this experience that I speak.

Your children have indomitable courage. They have and are standing up to burdens that have floored lesser men.

As our world grows more complex and the need for an adequate education becomes more acute, it is obvious that we need new miracles. The miracle of a fourth-grade education will not do. There are no jobs for fourth graders any more and, even if there were, they would not be the kind of jobs you would want for your child.

We believe that communication is the key to unlocking the potentialities of the deaf. And when we speak of communication we mean free and easy communication that will have the opportunity to grow as we grow, change as we change and continue to evolve until something develops that will be the best possible means we can devise.

This will not happen overnight. It may never come about at all unless the parents of deaf children accept their child's handicap and strive to give him the skills and strengths he needs to overcome this disability rather than try to make him an "imitation hearing man." You have such an opportunity here. I pray you make the most of it. It will take the best efforts of all of you, parents, teachers and counselors alike. And we want you to realize the whole world will be watching to decide for once and for all that it really is wiser to build a fence on top of the cliff rather than maintain ambulances down in the valley.

The Idiot—or Some of My Best Friends are Hearing

Speech delivered to the Manassas (Virginia) Lions Club, Spring, 1970. The reference in the first sentence to "this article" suggests that Fred intended it for publication; however, if it has been published, the journal is not known to this editor.

I would say that this article has been a long time in the writing. Partly this has been because it was and is difficult to believe that one needed it. Partly, too, because, as the title implies, what I have to say is not designed to win friends and influence people. Still, it seems that when all is said and done the time has come for the people in the field of deafness to take a good look at where they are and what they are advocating.

For the past decade there has been a gradual change in attitudes relative to methodology and particularly to the shopworn adage that deaf people must become imitation hearing people, because we have to live in a hearing world. As has frequently been noted, no one is quite sure what kind of a world those deaf oral failures live in. As far as I know, there are two schools of thought: the first is that all the oral failures live in a world of their own surrounded by a high picket fence. The second is that we all die 24 hours after we leave school. Unfortunately, neither supposition is correct. We do live in a hearing world. We walk the same streets that hearing people use. We go to the same stores. Our doctors and dentists do not discriminate and do treat hearing people, also. We pay taxes like hearing people do, and if the truth must be told, we go to the same jails they do when the occasion requires. But all of this obsession with the hearing world prompts one to inquire, What's so great about the hearing world anyway?

Obviously, this is an irreverent question and ought to be treated with the contempt it deserves. But if one takes the question in the same context in which the claims for the hearing world are made, it is not as idiotic as it seems. The world as we know it is dominated by people who hear. And one can see merely by looking at the headlines in the papers that it is in a *hell* of a *mess*. There is hardly a thing to indicate that hearing people are doing a great job in managing the world we live in. In fact, there is a great deal in the papers that leads one to think that one might, if he had a choice, do better than to choose this world. It is safe to say that all the wars in the world were started by people who hear; 99 and 44/100ths of all the crimes are committed by people who hear; and the same is true of all the vehicular homicides. Truly, there is little to support the desirability of living in the world of the hearing.

If I have not provided sufficient indictments of hearing people, let me add the crowning touch—all the silly TV commercials are also written by people who hear!

In a more serious vein, but not much more so, let me note also that for professionals who insist that the deaf be able to communicate with the rest of the hearing world, you have managed nobly to ignore the fact that hearing people have more difficulty in communicating with each other than we have. Nations are noted for their inability to communicate with nations. The young and the "over '30s" have an acknowledged communication gap; youth and law enforcement people have communication problems. Why do you want to inflict all of these things upon the deaf person who to some extent is isolated from all of this? Why is there such a determined effort to make hearing a virtue instead of the accident of birth that it is? Far too many deaf people have for too long been given the impression that they should equate hearing with intelligence, that people who hear are smart. But we all know that, in reality, there are as many stupid hearing people as there are smart ones. In fact, there are more stupid ones than there are smarties. However, I do not recall any emphasis on the point that ears are cheap. There are at least 200 million people in this country who have usable ears. But what is between those ears is different. In many cases there are people whose heads are used simply to separate the ears. In other cases the head is only a place where one hangs one's hat. None of which is given to the deaf individual.

Possibly the strangest of all is the fact that in this country we have earth-shaking decisions made by one man—that literally hundreds of decisions coming from the United States Supreme Court which have profound impact on the lives of all American citizens are made by a one-vote majority. People in this country, as good democrats, accept the rule for the majority, never questioning the right or wrong of it. But as far as deafness is concerned, everyone cheerfully ignores the fact that the vast majority of deaf people reject, and have consistently rejected for these 100 years, the oral philosophy. Doesn't this mean anything? Do professionals really believe they are God reincarnated? Do people really think that a "father knows best" attitude will get them anywhere? Granted there are times when the professional might have cures that are unknown to the patient and treatments that appear at times to be remote from the ailment. But after 100 years of rejection of oral "medicine" someone should have gotten the message.

A few days ago I was at a workshop in which the usual platitudes were flowing freely. One of the particular hackneyed phrases I was being exposed to was that sign language was a crutch. And it occurred to me then that of all the handicapped people only the deaf were denied their crutches. I want to reiterate as I have once before that there is nothing wrong with crutches. The blind have their canes, guide dogs and braille; amputees today have prosthetics; and paraplegics and quadripledgics have a variety of crutches which help them function normally or as near normal as their disabilities will permit. Anyone who is familiar with the marvelous advances in prosthetics might do well to ask themselves—if the amputees had been denied their crutches in early times, would these prosthetics exist today? After all, the arguments that one uses for the deaf are equally applicable for any other handicap. This is also a *seeing world*. The people who live in it can see. Therefore, the blind should not be permitted canes or dogs or braille. This is also a world where people have two legs and two arms. Amputees will have to compete with two-legged and two-armed animals. Therefore, they must learn to make their one arm or leg serve as well as two.

I know I am being ridiculous. But the arguments that are used on deafness are ridiculous. Why are they taken so seriously? Why is it that the hearing world is given such a mysticism that some parents and even some deaf youngsters are so cruelly misled as to completely blow their minds? I read, a few years back, a letter from a student at Bethany College to his alma mater. This student noted that he had transferred from Bucknell University to Bethany because Bucknell has proven to be too large, too impersonal for him to succeed. But he was doing well in Bethany. He said—and these words have been written in letters of fire in my brain— "Of course, I have to copy notes in class to keep from falling asleep." But he was obviously proud that he was going to a college for the hearing. So much so that the fact that he might as well have gone to the movies completely escaped him. What is so great about going to a college for the hearing, if all you can do is copy notes to keep from falling asleep?

Another young man in writing about his college career noted that he, too, was attending a college for the hearing but was "fortunate" in being excused from attending classes. Again, the question is What is fortunate about that? More importantly, what was done to this young man that he thought getting a piece of paper from a college for the hearing was worth all the money he was throwing away for an education he could have gotten in the public library? And what is even more important, who did the brainwashing that created such an attitude that completely ignored reality? This is the most serious question. Who is doing the brainwashing? How do the people who put so much emphasis on the virtues of hearing account for the fact that no matter what they do and no matter how hard they try to isolate the deaf child from his peers, at least 90 percent of all deaf people marry other deaf persons? A good number of deaf people do get into what is laughingly called the mainstream of life. In many cases these are people whose sensibilities have been so dulled that they are boors and so self-centered that they expect the world to revolve around them. They demand that the hearing community subordinate itself to their handicap and refuse to recognize that they are seldom truly welcomed anywhere. Others find themselves islands in this mainstream of hearing, lonely and isolated, not knowing that there are ways and means of bridging this loneliness and consoling themselves like the saints who wore hair shirts with the knowledge that they "made it", even though they are not quite sure why or if it was worth the suffering.

Truly, we have some strange attitudes. We note, for instance, that there is a concentrated effort to explain to people who hear what it means to be deaf. We do not see anyone explaining to the deaf person what it means, although it seems to me that if anyone would need to understand what deafness is all about it is the deaf person. There is no reason in the world to assume that, just because one is deaf, he understands it. In fact, there ought to be every reason in the world to see a need to explain to the deaf person the idiosyncracies of people who hear and why things happen the way they do in this not so wonderful world of the hearing. For example, one of the most noted difficulties of deaf people is that we think we are being "picked on." In many cases we are. But at work, as often as not, the fact is that we only get what we deserve but, because we cannot hear, we are not truly aware that the boss picks on our co-workers as well. We do not hear him chewing out the guy on the next machine, so we do not know that we are not the only ones who get bawled out. And no one explained to us that this happens. No one explains to us either why when at times we order coke we get coffee or why so few people seem to understand the "excellent speech" our teachers told us we had. It could very well be that these are trivial things to you, but they are important to us. Not understanding undermines our confidence. We did not have too much confidence to begin with, because of your insistence that we do everything the hardest possible way. We don't speak well— and despite all the praise and smiles and pats on the head, we know it. We may not admit that we know it, but even a dumb deaf kid knows that something is wrong when nobody understands what he is saying. Our language isn't so hot either, and we know that, too. We have a long history of failure before we even start out on our own and as Eddie Guest used to say:

"I see what others may never see,
I know what others may never know
I can never hide myself from me
So I want to be fit for myself to know."

What a Deaf Jewish Leader Expects of a Rabbi

This speech was published in Workshops on Orientation of Jewish Religious
Leaders and Laymen to Deafness and Vocational Rehabilitation. *Washington,
D.C.: United States Department of Health, Education and Welfare, 1970.*

To say what a deaf leader expects of a rabbi is an occasion made for
platitudes. I could discuss for hours all the characteristics of a rabbi which
are common demands of everyone, whether he is deaf or not. As a matter
of fact, the main point here is not what the deaf leader expects of a rabbi,
but rather what he thinks the deaf Jew needs and wants from his rabbi,
and this is somewhat more complex. Speaking from my own experiences
as a deaf Jew, there are a number of things which appear to stand out
as strong problems where religious matters are concerned.

The first of these is the lack of an adequate religious education. There
are only one or two schools for the deaf in this country that have any
relation to the Jewish faith and even in these schools the opportunities
available to the child to learn about his own religion are minimal. Being
raised in the Jewish faith at home does not do much to solve the problem.
The deaf child needs the same opportunity to learn the hows and whys
of his faith as does any other child. He needs not only religious instruction, but also explanations as to why things are not always the way they
should be. He needs to know why, for example, he does not always go
home from school on Rosh Hashonna nor fast on Yom Kippur. He needs
to know why his food is Kosher at home but not in school. But most of
all he needs to feel that his faith has a deep and abiding interest in him
and his welfare and that his rabbi is his teacher, his counselor, his source
of comfort and advice in times of distress.

Deaf people live in a world that differs vastly from any other because
the common medium that binds most people together is communication.
Our world is an auditory one, and the inability to learn by auditory methods imposes a heavy burden on the individual which, so far, has proven
barely tolerable. Helen Keller once noted that if she had to do it all over
again she would devote her time to working with the deaf
because"blindness cuts you off from things, while deafness cuts you off
from people."

It is this isolation that needs to be broken down and it is in this area
that the rabbi can be of most help. A good Christian friend of mine once
told me that it is impossible for a deaf person to fully integrate into the
world of the hearing. This man had good speech, good lip-reading ability
and he said: "I tried this (integration) in my church. I felt that if I could
succeed anywhere, that would be the place because in church, people are
consciously kind."

63

Whether or not my friend is correct is immaterial for this paper. The point is that there are very few avenues through which any deaf person can get sympathetic understanding and help for his problems. The deaf Jew needs to have someone to turn to in times of stress, someone who can counsel him, comfort him, guide him not only in religious matters, but with secular problems as well.

Most communities have an abundance of social service agencies which cover the entire spectrum of human needs. But if the Washington Community Survey is any indication, none of these agencies are equipped to deal with deaf persons. Few have personnel who can even communicate with deaf people. Even fewer have people whose knowledge of the psychology of deafness, the educational background and childhood development of the congenitally deaf person is adequate enough for effective counseling.

When the deaf Jew needs help, can he go to his rabbi and get it? Right now the answer must be "no". But he ought to be able to do so. What's more, the concept of seeking help from this source should be instilled in early childhood, so that when one grows older, one will instinctively think of one's rabbi in times of stress.

This, of course, poses problems. Few rabbis are any more familiar with the deaf than are the social service agencies mentioned previously. It may be unrealistic to expect that every rabbinical student be required to familiarize himself with what is an admittedly complex subject when the chances that he will have deaf people in his congregation are minimal to say the least. Still, it is not unreasonable to suggest that such students be advised to seek help from more knowledgeable people before attempting to give guidance, should the need arise. The deaf person can quickly recognize that his advisor is not familiar with the complexities of his disability and turn away, rejecting not only the advice but the advisor and perhaps even the Temple itself.

It does not seem far-fetched to suggest that rabbis be alerted to this problem and advised that the National Congress of Jewish Deaf be contacted as soon as one discovers there are deaf Jews in one's congregation. Then the Congress could provide lists of referral agencies and other sources of information that are available to the rabbis. Such professional help as psychiatrists, interpreters, social workers, etc., is available and can be secured when needed.

Where there are deaf Jews in a congregation the rabbi might assume a major role between the deaf person and community service agencies. In particular, the State's Vocational Rehabilitation Agency and the counselor assigned to the deaf person. While Rehabilitation Agency counselors may know a little more about deafness than the average rabbi, generally this is only a smidgen more and the counselor, over-burdened with a heavy caseload to begin with, cannot give his deaf client the time and attention he needs. But a rabbi could—he has, generally speaking, few handicapped people in his congregation and even fewer who need the kind of help the deaf individual requires. Thus, working with a Vocational Rehabilitation counselor, the rabbi could do much to help that counselor provide real service to his client. He might be able to ease communication difficulties, help with some of the formalities involved in processing a case, such as making medical appointments, hearing tests, or whatever is needed to help the client.

Religious leadership is another area where one would hope that the rabbis might exert a positive force. In my own community in Metropolitan Washington, there are enough Jews for at least special services on occasions such as Rosh Hashonna, Yom Kippur and Passover. This situation exists in other communities as well, but such services are seldom held. One might wonder why don't the deaf people themselves move in this direction? And that would be a valid question. The answer might be, first, that we have never received any encouragement to do so. Then there is the problem of communication; a deaf Jew can't just pick up a telephone and find a Temple or a rabbi who is willing and able to arrange for such services, nor can he easily reach the other members of his faith to convey the information. Finally, the quality of leadership varies from community to community so that truly effective leadership on the local level is scarce. Most deaf people are underemployed so that even the community leaders are severely restricted in what they can do; all are volunteers with very limited resources.

These are but a few of the things one expects from one's rabbi. Perhaps a great deal of attention should be focused on the children of the deaf. They are seldom considered, but they have a far-reaching effect on Judiasm. All evidence has shown that the deaf Jew has been sadly neglected by his religion. How, then, can he be a functioning member of his own congregation and also insure that his hearing children will be brought up in the faith of his fathers?

When I tried to enroll my children in Sunday School in Montgomery County where I live, I was told I had to be a member of the congregation, and despite my pointing out that I would derive no benefit from such membership, I was told "it would make my children feel better" if I joined. So I joined. I asked only that my children's teachers be made aware that I was deaf and did not have the training necessary to fulfill the role of a typical Jewish father. This did no good because my children were continually coming home with questions that their teachers had told them to "ask their father." These questions, of course, I could not answer, which embarrassed both me and my children. So I refused to continue as a member of this congregation and took my problem to a Reformed Temple hoping for more understanding. Here I was told by the rabbi that he was more interested in me than in my children. But I knew at that time there was little he could do for me, although, if my children had proper training, proper contacts, it was possible, even probable, that when they grew older they could interpret for me at the Services and thus bring me back in the fold. Since this was not to be, I had a private tutor to complete their religious education because it was never a matter of cost but rather of principle that motivated my actions. My sons were Bar Mitzvah but they never really had the social or religious contacts which lead to regular attendance at any Temple. At this time, two of my children have married Gentiles. The other two will probably do the same. This hurts. Whether he attends a Temple or not, whether he is deaf or not, a Jewish boy who grows up in a Jewish household, is still a Jew. And I began to wonder—how many families are there in the same situation as I? If the deaf Jew is not important to the Temple, certainly his children and his children's children should be and their future is worth considering.

Larger cities have deaf congregations. New York, Philadelphia, Chicago, Los Angeles, all boast of congregations of deaf people. All have regular services for deaf Jews and some may even make provision for the children of their members, but not enough is being done, not for the hearing children of deaf parents, not for the deaf children who live in all parts of the country, not just in the big cities and even in the cities where there are deaf congregations, all too often the impact is lost by the use of lay readers, interpreters and the like. The deaf Jew is reasonable enough to understand why an interpreter might be needed where only a few deaf people are involved. We do not really believe that every rabbi should or would learn to communicate with us in our own language, but we do think that where the congregation is large enough this should be done. We should be able to get rabbis who are thoroughly familiar with all aspects of deafness, who can communicate with us in our own language, and who can instill in us a feeling of trust and security.

For our deaf children, there should be a more intensified effort to see to it that they get proper religious training. It is disheartening to note that when reading over the literature on education, there is, if not frequent, at least regular mention of what is available for Christians—and almost nothing—I say almost to be conservative because I have found nothing at all—about programs for Jews. I don't care whose fault this is and I would not even want to speculate on whose responsibility it is to insure that something is done to provide our deaf Jewish children with adequate religious training. It seems to me that if religion is important, then it is the responsibility of those primarily concerned with religion to see to it that the children are not neglected.

It is fairly certain that there is at least one Temple located in those communities that contain residential schools for the deaf. Many of these schools may have only a few Jewish children but they are there. For the most part the children, perhaps, are enroute between the school and their homes on Fridays; they generally live too far from the school to return to their homes for the holidays; Jewish holidays that is; so they get no attention at all. Why can't the Temple take the initiative in seeing to it that the children get adequate training? I am sure school administrations would cooperate, and that interpreters could be found to assist the rabbis in this important task if it were undertaken. When one stops to consider that it is not only the deaf child who is being lost to Israel, but also his children and his children's children, the effort necessary appears justified. After all, aren't we *all* the Lord's Chosen People?

The Obvious?

Reprinted from Guest Lecture Series, *published by North Carolina School for the Deaf, Morganton, 1971.*

It is with great pleasure that I am here today. With so many things going on, it is difficult to choose a subject that would do justice for the occasion, and the only thing that seems to make sense at this time is to do what I know best—to try to give the consumer's point of view about what is happening in our world today and what we think is going to happen or should happen. I believe that this is known in the vernacular as "doing one's thing."

Originally I had intended to choose as my topic a remark which was made by one of the participants at the Fort Monroe Workshop on Community Development back in 1961, which was the start of the decade known as the Golden Sixties, as far as programs for the deaf are concerned. At that time, a Mr. Clifford Horton said, "Never overlook the obvious—what may be obvious to you may not be so obvious to the rest of us." This seemed to be a good theme, because we find this especially true in the area of education, and it seemed entirely possible that our educators have been overlooking the obvious in their research for better ways of educating deaf children.

A short time later, however, I was forcibly reminded that there was something much more drastically wrong with our situation which could not be covered by the foregoing. This was at the Convention of the Professional Rehabilitation Workers with the Adult Deaf. During the course of this meeting I listened to speakers reiterate time and time again about the problems of communication in relation to services for their clients. At that time I was reminded that I had attended at least 100 meetings in the past decade, meetings of parents, mental health experts, rehabilitation workers, religious workers, and what have you, and all through these meetings there was that one recurrent theme "Communication." As I listened, I was struck anew with the fact that on the campuses of our schools for the deaf today there are rehabilitation counselors; that we are preparing to rehabilitate our students before they were even habilitated and that despite all the complaints from the rehabilitation workers we are continuing to turn out more of the same year after year. As I looked back over what had been said in the past, I was struck by the fact that we all appear to be talking to ourselves. I have listened to this stuff for the past ten years and yet how many people are sitting up and taking notice of what is going on? Do educators speak to rehabilitation workers? And what is more important, do they listen? Do rehabilitation workers speak to educators, and if not, why not? Why do psychiatrists, who certainly know the fundamental facts of psychology, use terms like "early communication" when they know that the parent and the educator will twist that to mean whatever they want it to mean? Why don't we call a spade a spade?

Some of you may be familiar with the paper I gave on the Adult Deaf Person's Point of View and particularly to the poem which I acknowledge having "borrowed" from Dr. Ray Jones, because it was the most appropriate poem for our situation that I have ever read. I am going to recite it here.

A FENCE OR AN AMBULANCE

By Joseph Malius

'Twas a dangerous cliff, as they freely confessed
Though to walk near its crest was so pleasant,
But over its terrible edge there had slipped,
A duke and full many a peasant.
So the people said something would have to be done,
But their projects did not at all tally.
Some said, "Put a fence round the edge of the cliff,"
Some, "An ambulance down in the valley."
But the cry for the ambulance carried the day,
For it spread through the neighboring city.
A fence may be useful or not, it is true,
But each heart became brimful of pity,
For those who slipped over that dangerous cliff;
And the dwellers in highway and alley
Gave pounds or gave pence, not to put up a fence
But an ambulance down in the valley.
"For the cliff is all right if you're careful," they said,
It isn't the slipping that hurts them so much,
As the shock down below when they're stopping.
So day after day, as these mishaps occurred,
Quick forth would their rescuers sally,
To pick up the victims who fell off the cliff
With their ambulance down in the valley.
Then an old sage remarked, "It's a marvel to me
That people give far more attention
To repairing results than to stopping the cause
When they'd much better aim at prevention.
Let us stop at its source all the mischief," he cried
"Come neighbors and friends let us rally.
If the cliff we will fence, we might almost dispense
With the ambulance down in the valley."
"Oh, he's a fanatic," the others rejoined,
"Dispense with the ambulance? Never.
He'd dispense with all charities too, if he could,
No, no, we'll support them forever.
Aren't we picking up folks just as fast as they fall
And shall this man dictate to us? Shall he?
Why should people of sense stop to put up a fence
While the ambulance works in the valley?"
But a sensible few who are practical too,
Will not bear with such nonsense much longer.
They believe that prevention is better than cure,
And their party will still be the stronger.
Encourage them then with your purse, voice and pen,
And while other philanthropists dally

They will scorn all pretense and put up a fence
On the cliff that hangs over the valley.
Better guide well the young than reclaim them when old,
For the voice of true wisdom is calling.
To rescue the fallen is good but 'tis best
To prevent other people from falling.
Better close up the source of temptation and crime,
Than deliver from dungeon and galley.
Better put a strong fence round the top of the cliff
Than an ambulance down in the valley.

I would like to submit to you that all the new programs we have initiated in the past decade, the Delgado College, the Model Secondary School, the increased services offered by rehabilitation agencies, all the plans we have for the decade ahead of us are simply more ambulances down in the valley. They indicate to the pragmatist that deaf people have been and are falling off the top of our cliffs faster than the ambulance we have stationed down in the valley can haul them off to the hospital—in this case, rehabilitation. We are saying we need more ambulances because it is certainly the right of every unfortunate to secure prompt attention whenever and as soon as he falls off the top of the cliff.

Being of the older generation, I do not subscribe to Charles Wilson's famous quote "What's good for General Motors is good for the country." And while I can easily concede that more ambulances down in the valley might be good for General Motors, this is a poor condolence for the people who are falling over the top of our educational cliffs in ever-increasing numbers. We should not need new programs we are getting or at least not so much as we need the kind of programs that will attack our problems at the source rather than remedy the damage that has already been done.

I am sure you are all as sick of methodology as I am. And I do not really want to bring up this hoary subject again, because as far as I am concerned, there is nothing that can be said about this that has not already been said. But I do want to point out that the experience of our rehabilitation counselors and our mental health workers ought to have some bearing on the matter, not to mention the fact that the vast majority of adult deaf people are overwhelmingly in favor of what is now called Total Communication.

It seems to me that education for the deaf is like an ostrich with its head in the sand and its posterior temptingly positioned so that it is difficult to be critical if one is tempted to place his foot where he thinks it will do the most good. This is true even though we are aware that few people in the field of service to the deaf are wholly without fault and hence are in no position to cast the first stone.

But to get back to my initial point of overlooking the obvious: What is education anyway? Do we have education, schools just for the sake of having them? Do we have schools for the deaf child merely to provide jobs for people who have nothing better to do? Or are there goals and, if there are, what the heck are they? The poor consumer, the product of our current educational system and probably his parents as well, is under the illusion (or maybe it is the delusion) that the purpose of education is to prepare one for life, "out in the world", as it is commonly said. We think that is what we are going to school for or that's what we went to school for, and it becomes somewhat disheartening to learn that a prominent educator of the deaf, when asked how her graduates were faring in the world of work, replied, "That's irrelevant!"

We want to submit to you that it is not irrelevant. It is the whole reason why we went to school, and it is the primary task of our educators to see to it that school graduates are as well prepared to take as high a place in our society as is possible. We would like to suggest that education as such has three broad aspects which must be fulfilled if the educator is to sit back and congratualte himself or herself on a job well done. These are:

1. To prepare the student for gainful employment. While this could easily be taken to mean to learn a trade, that is not what we have in mind. We refer to prevocational training, social and personal adjustment, the needs and requirements which are axiomatic, if the individual is to be employable. Job skills can be taught anytime and anywhere, but the other aspects of the world of work must be taught within the school system.

2. To prepare the student to assume his responsibilities to society and the community in which he lives. It is our experience that most graduates from a school for the deaf consider themselves apart from the mainstream of community living. They do not feel any particular obligation to their communities or even their nation. They have no sense of responsibility to their own organizations much less to those of the community at large. Yet the responsibility of voting and taking part in community affairs to whatever degree they are able ought to be instilled in them while they are still in school.

3. To prepare the student to enjoy the fruits of his labor. It seems to me that this point is perhaps the most critical of all. When all is said and done, labor per se has no meaning. A horse works for a living, but we are not horses. It is the rewards of work that differentiate man from the rest of the animals. We can find no value in the suggestion that, if we forego all of our pleasures and concentrate on getting into step with the majority of the nation, we will perhaps advance higher on the monetary scale than if we are able to enjoy whatever it is that we are working for in the first place. There may be some mysterious virtue in being integrated in the hearing world and miserable, because the only kind of integration we understand is social integration and we know that social integration never works. But if there is some virtue, tell us what it is. "Man does not live by bread alone" is a hoary saying. Does it not apply to the deaf person as well as to those who can hear? Is it not more important that one can derive pleasure from books, from a solid command of his mother tongue, rather than the mere ability to mouth words?

Is there not more comfort in being able to go home to ones family and feel "at home" with them, at ease with the world and to accept what is on our own terms? We think so. We think it is much more desirable to be a non-speaking teacher of the deaf than an oral janitor. Or for that matter, an oral mechanical engineer who has only his work to keep him company.

We think it is the responsibility of educators to go out into the world and ascertain what their former pupils are doing, to assess how well the education they imparted is being utilized, and to make whatever changes that are necessary to provide the future school graduate with the kind of education that will best serve his needs. We are well aware that no school can be all things to all men, but we also think that education must give us the tools to help us build ourselves a better life—the kind of life that we can face with confidence and can build upon.

We believe it is the responsibility of the educator to tell it like it is. No doubt parents may not like what you have to tell them; they may even raise a ruckus about it, but one cannot always hide from reality. Nor can one shirk ones responsibilities, because the results may be unpleasant. Parents have the right to know just what is in store for their children. They have the right to an honest assessment of their child's potential and his chances for success. If educators don't give it to them, who will? Who can? How does one live with oneself when the normal deaf child turns out to be a functionally illiterate adult? How does one reconcile oneself to switching a child from an oral environment to a manual one after all hope of reaching his true potential has been eliminated? These are questions you have to ask yourself. We have no doubt that many parents cannot, will not, accept this kind of advice, but like the thousands of people with incurable diseases who go from quack to quack hoping for a miracle they will persist in seeking "normalcy." Some of them may even find that miracle, but to sacrifice 75-90 percent of our young people for the sake of the remaining few is a high price to pay for miracles. It is an especially high price when it has never been truly proven that the remaining 10-25 percent cannot or will not manage to do whatever it is that oral education is supposed to do, because they were exposed at a tender age to Total Communication.

I am all too well aware that there is a tendency to suggest by some very respected authorities, as well as by the deaf themselves, that given Total Communication all our problems will be solved. I know that this is not so. I am sure that many problems will remain even after we have reconciled our differences in this particular area of methodology. But I cannot help but feel that once this has been reconciled we will be able to focus our attention on these problems which are now hidden in the forests of controversy over methods. It will only be then that we can turn our attention to meeting the very real needs and very special needs of the deaf child. Until we honestly and truly come to grips with the simple question, is the child deaf or is he not, we will continue to spend all our time building ambulances down in the valley rather than fences on the top of our cliffs.

I dare to suggest that every school for the deaf needs two or more deaf consumers on its school board if the school has one. The schools also need parent representation on the same board if this is at all possible. Where it is not possible, perhaps because the school has no board of its own or has an elected board, then the school should seek to establish some kind of advisory group which would include the representation mentioned above. I am so bold as to suggest that this idea is not novel nor unique. The entire concept was built into our democratic system. School boards all over the nation are made up of laymen, not professional educators. They are composed of persons whose experience in non-educational areas qualifies them to determine the needs of their local school system. Where the deaf are concerned, their experience is unique in that they are the only ones who have and are living with the day-to-day realities of having non-functional hearing in a hearing world. Their day-to-day experience is what is really needed to enable education to apply its expertise to meet the crisis that we are experiencing and to offer solutions to the problems we encounter. Education never was intended to dwell in ivory towers; that it has, no one can doubt, and that its inclination to maintain the status quo is responsible for all the unrest that we are experiencing on the campuses of our institutions of higher learning today has been well documented. Relevance is a battle cry of people who are tired of irrelevance, of mythology, of people so far from the scene that they don't even recognize advance when it comes up and hits them in the face.

Priority Needs of Deaf People

A telephone lecture to the Leadership Training Program, at San Fernando Valley State College, February 25, 1971.

Originally, the theme suggested for this discussion was "Unmet Needs of Deaf People." This, however, would have been very limiting, because the unmet needs of deaf people include everything. It is safe to say that nowhere are the needs of deaf persons being adequately taken care of. It is equally safe to say that these needs will never be adequately handled unless the consumer and the professionals get together on a system of priorities that will eliminate needless duplication, focus more effort on immediate needs and involve more direct action toward achieving our goals.

When one compares the array of services which are available to persons with normal hearing to those available to the hearing handicapped, the vast difference can easily substantiate what has been said that none of the needs of the deaf population are being adequately met.

To correct this condition, perhaps the most urgent priority is to establish priorities and delineate areas of responsibility. Considering that I am offering a priority listing today, this may sound redundant. Still, a workable priority list cannot be developed by one man, perhaps not even by a dozen men. It must result from mutual agreement by all the people in the field, consumer, parent, professional, and what have you. In my opinion, this is the true purpose of the Council of Organizations Serving the Deaf. The Council, involving as it does all the organizations of and for the deaf in this country, is the ideal vehicle for the establishment of these priorities and for the co-ordination of effort that will be necessary to achieve the objectives thus set forth.

It seems obvious that efficient action will mean that whatever the area in which priorities are established, more than one agency will be involved, a primary agency, perhaps, and a number with secondary roles, co-ordinated within that priority by the primary agency with the overall co-ordinating role, the role of meeting priorities handled by the COSD itself.

The second priority would be resolution of the controversy on methodology. The oral-total-communication battle lies as a festering sore over the entire efforts for increasing opportunities for deaf people. I wonder how many millions of dollars have been spent in a futile effort to repair the damages created by methodology. When one reads the literature in the field, and takes into consideration the vast amounts of money spent trying to determine whether this or that method is best, then adds the reports from professionals in other areas (the rehabilitation workers, mental health people, employment and placement counselors) we wonder if there are any rational people left in the world.

Considering the profound and far-reaching effects of the methdological problem it seems to me that a massive effort would be justified to determine—not at the school level, but at the adult level—the true effect of our differences. I am not a researcher and thus cannot suggest methodology for such a study, but I do know the deaf people, the rehabilitation counselors, the psychiatrists, etc., who work with the deaf have a story to tell which should be listened to and acted upon. I know, too, that there is more to be found behind the recurrent "hearing world" theme than shows on the surface. Is it true that speech, etc., is essential for advancement, or are we really being defeated by the expectations we have been creating in the minds of employers on the efficacy of speech and speech-reading? If we can resolve this problem, we would have more time, more money, more people able to focus on the real needs of education and employment of deaf persons than we have now.

The third priority might be called a long-range one. I am somewhat naive and tend to fall back on relatively unsophisticated courses of action. For example, I believe in beginning at the beginning. This means to me an early-identification system. We are all agreed that the sooner we identify the child with a hearing loss, the better we are able to help that child and minimize the consquences of such loss. We must have a nationwide, workable means of doing this and as fast as we can get it. I am brash enough to suggest that perhaps the primary agency for such an activity might be the American Speech and Hearing Association, with a secondary role allotted the Deafness Research Foundation in seeing to it that the medical profession is alerted, not only to the symptoms that presage hearing loss, but also to the consequences of procrastination. I am sure the other organizations would have a role here, but cannot at this time offer concrete suggestions.

Fourth should be a revision of our educational program. However, this would be dependent on the other priorities, so that it might be held in abeyance, because both the methodology and identification problems have yet to be resolved.

Fourth, then, would be in the area of training. One needs no reminder that, except for rehabilitation counseling, there are virtually no professionals trained to serve deaf people. So far as I am aware, the number of social workers qualified to work with the deaf can be counted on one hand. This is equally true in the mental health field, the medical, legal, and nursing professions. One is compelled to note that within the Social and Rehabilitation Services there are seven separate administrations, only one of which provides any kind of training services for the deaf, and that is the Rehabilitation Services Administration. We have a Community Services Administration, Administration on the Aging, a Welfare Administration. But are these programs meeting our needs? I would say no.

I must say that the needs for social workers and mental health workers is greater than even for administrators or educators, and somewhere along the line these needs must be met.

Fifth would be protection of the legal rights of deaf citizens. There has been frequent mention of the needs for special laws to protect deaf people; I do not agree. It seems to me that the laws of our land are adequate for our needs. Our problem is in seeing to it that these laws are interpreted correctly, so that the deaf person's rights are safeguarded. It is ironic that the Supreme Court upholds the right of people to disseminate what we often consider rank pornography on the basis of the First Amendment to the Constitution but does not extend to the deaf child the right to learn through any method he or his parents might desire. It becomes downright ridiculous when our courts free confessed criminals on the grounds that their rights were not fully explained to them, but make no provision to insure that these same rights are fully explained and understood by deaf persons in similar situations. We have laws in our land which require drivers to have auto insurance but no laws that require insurance companies to provide this insurance. There are laws that provide special assistance to people who use other foreign languages but few such laws are on the books requiring interpreters for the deaf. Yet, if one agrees that sign language is a language, it must follow that it should be covered by the same laws that cover other foreign languages. This seems to be a task for the NAD and the PRWAD.

Sixth: Parent Education. When one is confronted with the fact that ones child is handicapped, it is necessarily a traumatic period, no matter what the handicap might be. When the handicap happens to be deafness, the problem is magnified. Most people have little more than a superficial knowledge of most disabilities, and where they do not, usually the medical profession can provide such parents with a place to start. But when the child is deaf, the doctor knows nothing, the audiologist only a little more, probably only enough to identify the degree and nature of the loss. So where does the bewildered parent go? Who can help him, and how does one find this help? One is invited to contact Associations for Mental Retardation, Blindness, Cerebral Palsy, Multiple Sclerosis, etc., daily via TV, radio spot announcements. Is the same true of hearing loss, particularly irreversible loss? If methodology were not in the way, the Bell Association, assisted by various religious denominations, might assume this task.

Seventh: Self-Image. If deaf people are to get ahead in our time, they must have a better image of themselves and their capabilities. They need concrete examples of what deaf people have already done so that they can project for themselves a brighter future. If we can have Black studies, Jewish studies, why not Deaf studies?

Eighth: Consumer Involvement. We have come a long way from the horse and buggy days when we coined the phrase, "You can lead a horse to the water, but you can't make him drink." However, the truth of this phrase is only now becoming evident in areas of social development and policy. Consumer participation on the policy-making level has just begun to have its value recognized. The Department of Health, Education and

Welfare, in setting up the National Citizens Conference, in 1969, tacitly was acknowledging that no matter how perfect a plan one devises, no matter how urgently it might be needed, nor how beneficial it might be, if the people for whom the program is intended do not want it, it is bound to fail. We have more consumer involvement today but still face the problem of separating the professional who is deaf from the consumer. Too many people tend to insist on the use of professionals in the place of consumers. This is wrong. While a deaf professional is probably closer to the consumer than one who is not deaf, he is still a professional, more concerned with what is needed in his field than what is wanted. He is a professional and should be considered as such.

Ninth: Mechanical Research. At least, I am calling it mechanical research if only to differentiate from social and psychological research. It does not quite make sense that a nation that has the engineering capability to put a man on the moon cannot use its electronic and mechanical skills to come up with gadgets, if you wish, that would ease some of the more awkward aspects of hearing loss. We have phonetypes and electrowriters; there supposedly exist soundscribers which are capable of transforming the spoken word into written language automatically. We need these things. We have the knowledge and technical skills to produce an infinite variety of devices that could compensate for hearing loss one way or another. But who is giving this any attention? All the devices we have were invented for other reasons and adapted to use by the deaf.

Tenth: Political Involvement. Pragmatically speaking, if the deaf are to get the kind of service they need and the protection they are entitled to under the laws of our country, they will have to become much more involved in politics than has been the case, heretofore. While I am not actively suggesting that we need to lobby, I do believe that we need to take a more aggressive role in making our needs known to our legislatures, particularly on the state and local level. I will immodestly state that we do better on the national level, but even here there is plenty of room for improvement. We should join forces with other groups when it is to our advantage to do so and use every bit of leverage we can muster to promote legislation that is favorable to our needs. For too long the deaf population has been given the impression that it is way too small to get anything but crumbs from the legislative table. We need to correct this impression and to make it clear that you don't get what you don't ask for, and you get what you do ask for, if you know who and how to ask.

I have selected just ten priorities and am calling them my Ten Commandments. There are many more items that I have not covered. However, if these ten commandments can be made realities, I believe the rest will be easy.

The Deaf Consumer Evaluates the HEW Potential for Deaf People

Speech to unknown workshop, sometime in 1971-1973.

When one attempts to cover a topic such as this, it is done with considerable misgivings. First, because it is a little presumptuous for us to attempt to evaluate HEW, and second, because there are many unmet needs of deaf people and many programs that, while not the direct responsibility of the Department of Health, Education and Welfare, are so closely related that one cannot help but feel that the Department should be far more involved in meeting these needs than is presently the case. In this context, this paper shall focus on some of these needs, for which we feel the potential of HEW might successfully be utilized.

At the same time, it must be recognized that HEW, and particularly its Rehabilitation Services Administration, has been more responsive to the needs of the deaf than any other administrative branch of our government. I wish very much to acknowledge this point before continuing. What follows could easily be taken to mean that we are unaware or unappreciative of all the support we have received and are receiving today. This is not the case, but our needs are so many and so varied that it appears that what we have only scratched the surface.

In the Social and Rehabilitation Services Administration there are at least three major divisions which we feel have great potential in meeting our needs. The first of these is the Rehabilitation Services Administration. While this administration has been the most active of all agencies where the deaf are concerned, and the Office of Deafness and Communicative Disorders has division status, that office is woefully understaffed with but two professional persons to handle the whole spectrum of communicative disorders. We feel that if the Office of Deafness is to adequately fulfill its responsibilities it will require a far larger staff than presently exists, and would urge that such an increased staff be forthcoming as expeditiously as possible. We believe there are many areas in which the Office could and should function, but does not. There are even some areas of need which are not directly related to the rehabilitative process to which we feel the Office of Deafness might relate. This concerns an advocacy role in connection with agencies in the federal structure, within and outside the Department of Health, Education and Welfare. Included here are, in particular, the Civil Service Commission and all agencies which operate under CSC regulations. We contend that CSC requirements for employment are unrealisitc where deaf people are concerned and that there is a lamentable lack of flexibility in allowing for the employment and advancement of deaf people. There are also cases of outright discrimination which either bar employment, or, if employed, advancement, where an effective advocate would be far more successful than we have been.

Inasmuch as the goal of the Rehabilitation Services Administration is the gainful employment of handicapped people at the highest levels of their abilities, it appears logical that charity should begin at home, and the RSA should be concerned with the barriers that are preventing deaf people from securing employment within the federal government. It is unrealistic to expect that the states and/or private industry can be influenced to increase substantially employment of the deaf when the Federal government does not. Further, most state and local civil service agencies are patterned after the CSC, and thus there are very, very few deaf persons employed by state and county governments. We look to RSA to work with the Civil Service Comimssion to develop more realistic testing methods and more flexibility in job descriptions so that the broad requirements incorporated in most descriptions will not needlessly bar deaf people from employment.

We look, also, to the RSA for more realistic and meaningful delivery of services. Again, we recognize that it is not the function of the Office of Deafness to provide direct services. However, on the regional and state levels, there is a paucity of persons knowledgeable of the needs of deaf people. Because of this lack of knowledge we are making little headway in meeting even the barest minimum of our needs. The number of trained rehabilitation counselors for the deaf is pitifully small. In many cases these counselors have general caseloads so that they are unable to provide adequately for their deaf clients, and some services that are authorized by law are not being provided. This lack of knowledge is so great that not even those programs which have been put into effect for other handicapped and disadvantaged persons are available to us; for example, the outreach program that is used with the disadvantaged. This program brings services to the client rather than depending on the client coming in for aid. Such a program is even more important to the deaf client than it is to the disadvantaged. Even as the disadvantaged are awed and discomforted at the prospect of venturing forth into the confines of officialdom, the deaf person, with his communicative difficulties, is overwhelmed.

We look forward to the placement of rehabilitation counselors in clubs for the deaf, at least one of which exists in each of our major cities. This would bring the counselor to the client in surroundings with which we are familiar and eliminate the formidable gauntlet of personnel that we have to run each time we venture forth into the wilderness of governmental offices. And by minimizing the terrors and frustration that many of us face in seeking help, increase the number of people rehabilitated each year.

Such a program would require more training, particularly in the area of communication. The SRS has supported the NAD's Communicative Skills Program for quite some time. However, this program operates with minimal staffing and could do much more if funds for staffing were available. Such an outreach program might also serve the elderly if regulations are flexible enough to permit it. And serving the deaf person in his own environment might permit the growth of true community centers which would enable the deaf citizen to make more use of existing private and public community resources. As we see it, the ultimate source of assistance for the multitude of human needs lies in the local community. The services are there. All that is really needed is the means by which these resources might be used.

Also within SRS is the Administration on Aging. There are literally millions of older people who suffer hearing loss. Some have always been that way. Others have become deaf as a result of the aging process. Yet there are no programs within the AOA that take into account the effect of hearing loss. What is worse, after considerable effort to focus attention on the problems and needs resulting from hearing loss among the elderly we succeed in getting the recommendations developed at a conference on the aged deaf included in the proceedings of the recent White House Conference on Aging. These recommendations were the result of a conference on needs of aged deaf people sponsored by the Deafness Research and Training Center, an SRS-supported agency. Yet, when follow-up questionnaires were sent out, there were references to programs for many different handicapping conditions, but not deafness. There are many programs in the AOA which have and are providing valuable assistance to our Senior Citizens. Few of them take into consideration the needs of the deaf. There are few homes for the aged to care for those deaf people who are unable to care for themselves. None of the homes receives more than token assistance from our government. These homes, incidentally, are for people who have been deaf most of their lives. If there are any homes that cater to those whose hearing loss came as a result of aging, I do not know of them. Yet, we desperately need adequate facilities for this purpose, including staffing. We feel we ought to be able to look to the AOA for help in meeting this need. We also need convalescent homes which might be combined with the homes for the aged. Where long periods of convalescence are indicated, the isolation experienced by a deaf patient not only retards healing but can also lead to mental health problems.

I am not sure which agency is directly concerned with mental health. I would like to point out, however, that mental health programs are virtually nonexistent. We have but two, both on the East coast, and we need at least 50. There are no training programs for mental health workers for the deaf, and no effort to consolidate the many deaf people now in general institutions for the mentally ill. Nor, for that matter, are there diagnostic services available to insure that all deaf people now in such instituions belong there. From time to time we have discovered perfectly normal deaf people in institutions for no other reason than that they were deaf. We suspect that there are large numbers of people like this, both in institutions for the mentally ill and for the mentally retarded who are there simply because of faulty diagnosis. Inasmuch as the relatively few deaf people in this country preclude establishment of appropriate diagnostic services on even a state-by-state basis, we look to the Department for solutions to this problem, and especially the problem of committing normal deaf people into institutions where they do not belong. The Rehabilitation Services Administration has funded many training programs for audiology and speech pathology. Could it not also fund programs to train mental health personnel?

Could it not, also, join the AOA in establishing outreach programs so that our Senior Citizens can also benefit from the programs now available to others?

The third division of SRS in the Community Services Administration. I must confess that I am barely aware of the CSA. This may indicate how little help deaf people are getting from that agency, if any. In a country where there are multiplicity of agencies to meet the needs of the hearing population, it is disheartening, to say the least, to realize how few agencies there are that adequately serve the deaf. It is even more disheartening to realize how little is being done to make the resources of these community agencies available to the deaf, although we feel sure there are reasonable and economically feasible ways of doing so. We look to the CSA to provide solutions to these needs.

I do not think time will permit me to cover all the other items in this area. But before I leave SRS, I would like to reiterate something we have suggested before: the establishment of a consumer committee or council that could provide meaningful input on the needs of the deaf. I believe that the aftermath of the White House Conference on Aging, as well as the lack of specific services from other parts of the Department, should clearly indicate that, without a continual focussing on the needs of the hearing impaired, we will continue to be overlooked and neglected.

With respect to the Office of Education, again we would acknowledge that, next to SRS, the Bureau of Education for the Handicapped has been the most responsive to our needs. We are most grateful and pleased with the efforts of Media Services and Captioned Films for the Deaf for the work that has been done. We have also gotten good support for certain other projects within BEH. However, there are areas in which we feel there is much room for improvement. We are concerned with the number of federally supported teacher-training programs. We believe that it would be more effective if there were fewer programs of higher quality than the present situation permits. We are also concerned by the fact that there are few deaf students in these programs and, where deaf students are accepted, the accepting institutions are penalized for accepting them. That is, there are no provisions for interpreters services to the centers. No allowances are made for the admittance of out-of-state students as must be the case where deaf applicants are concerned, thus putting an immeasurable burden on state facilities. Inasmuch as the purpose of education is to prepare the student for a useful life in our society, we cannot help but feel that training centers should not only be encouraged to accept deaf students, but also given every inducement to make it attractive for them to do so. In allocating support for training, priority should be given to those institutions who do accept deaf students.

Vocational education offers another area of concern. We applaud the increased interest of junior colleges in making postsecondary education available to us. We are also interested in quality education but there does not seem to be any criteria in determining what constitutes a quality program. There are only minimal, if any, criteria for faculty and staff. It seems to us that, in many instances, all that is provided for deaf students are interpreters and note takers. We submit that it requires more than this to effectively serve the deaf and believe that hard and fast criteria should be established to insure that the deaf student is not short-changed. Further, there are, at present, three—four, if one includes the National Technical Institute for the Deaf—quality programs that provide post-secondary education for the deaf. While we agree that these are not enough, we also feel that indiscriminate proliferation of programs can be detrimental not only to the students but to the good programs as well.

Perhaps most frustrating of all is the fact that there are, within the Department, numerous programs which are applicable to the deaf but are not used, sometimes due to lack of knowledge, sometimes due to the inflexibility of administrating agencies and/or the actual wording of the law. The Higher Education Act of 1968 has provisions for supporting services to the disadvantaged, including the deaf. We are particularly interested in this, because, under the provisions of the law and the demonstrated interest of Congress, the funding of interpreters and note takers could be achieved. The Act, since it was written for larger minorities than the deaf, calls for applications from institutions for this purpose. This is a very cumbersome way to do this when a college has but one or two students needing this kind of assistance. And the time and effort required to do this are too great for the expected return. One might also wonder what would happen to the Office of Higher Education if every college and University accepting deaf students were to apply. Yet when the Registry of Interpreters for the Deaf, an organization supported by SRS, applied for funds for this purpose, its application was rejected because "grants are made directly to the institutions." If the institutions did apply, there would be no problem, but they don't, except perhaps those with relatively large enrollments, and we are forced to fall back on Vocational Rehabilitation funds and, if provided, that limits what Vocational Rehabilitation can do in other areas. The whole point here is that the money is available. If the records of the hearings on this act can be believed, Congress intended that the deaf be included, and we are not.

This also applies to Continuing Education. More than any other group of people, the deaf need continuing education programs, programs that are geared to our special needs. We are cut off, both by our limited reading skills and our disability, from traditional sources of information, as represented by mass media, and prevented from utilizing regular adult education programs either by our inability to benefit from them or, where special classes can be formed, by our numbers, which create difficulties in finding the required minimum number of students to form a class. There are also other problems, such as the lack of interpreters or local regulations that serve to prevent qualified people skilled in communication from teaching. Again, Congress intended that such a program be established, even appropriated funds for the purpose, but the money has not been released and the program is far from operational.

In the area of health, we have many programs—excellent programs, I might say. There are literally hundreds of them, none of which are used by us. We have Drug Abuse programs which are lavishly funded, but none for the deaf. We have Child Health and Maternity programs, but none for the deaf. There are Family Planning projects, and on down the line.

These programs ought to be available to us. The trouble is the NAD is the only consumer organization we have, and we have enough resources to know what we are missing, but not enough to do anything about them. In fact when we do seek support from the government to remedy certain situations, the cost-sharing requirement works against us and severely limits our efforts. Yet a Drug Abuse program is badly needed. While the problem has not yet reached epidemic proportions, it is growing, and one should not wait until it becomes overwhelming before deciding to act.

I have purposely omitted all mention of research heretofore, because I wish to treat this as a unit without regard to applicable agencies. It seems to us that not enough effort is put into long-term research. It would appear incredible that we have no accurate count of the number of deaf people in the United States. Even more incredible is the lack of information on the characteristics of the deaf population. This appears to be a vital need that is only being half-met now with the support of SRS for the National Census of the Deaf. We should have at least annual surveys that will permit an indepth examination of the characteristics of the deaf adult. How can one effectively educate a deaf child without knowing his needs? How do you train boys and girls for employment without knowing what kind of employment is available? How do you open up new areas of employment when you don't know which ones are now closed? These questions must be researched and answered if the maximal delivery of services is to be achieved.

There are many areas of research that have not been explored, especially where long-term research is concerned. What research do we have on visual learning? On eye care for people who depend entirely on their eyes for living? We have research into architectural barriers. Do we have research into visual barriers? It seems inconceivable that a nation that has the technical knowledge to put a man on the moon is unable either to bridge the gap from the ear to the brain or come up with equipment that will do so. Do we have research on mechanical ears? Or on devices that will convert the spoken word into visual symbols? This kind of research can be meaningful and could possibly eliminate the communication barriers which appear to be the underlying cause of most, if not all, our problems. Is there any research program on the prevention of deafness? I know we have immunization programs for rubella, whooping cough and other diseases which once caused deafness, but these are not primarily concerned with prevention.

These are but a few of the unmet needs of deaf people for which HEW has great potential to solve. Strictly speaking, I have more or less limited myself to areas that appeared to be wholly within the scope of my topic. I have refrained from discussing the inequities in the telephone rate structure, or the problems of television and transportation, even though all these might very well be related, since all these have a direct effect on employment.

I have refrained also from discussing welfare, largely because deaf people are proud people, and little is said within the community on this subject. However, the problems here are similar to those in the other agencies and specifically the communication difficulties which create hardships for the deaf because when welfare regulations were written no thought was given to people who cannot use the phone, who lack any means of communication other than direct contact. Where there are deaf people on welfare, we can't find them. If they are referred to Vocational Rehabilitation offices, I am not aware of it. I am aware that when an unemployed person who may or may not be a welfare client reports to the United States Employment Services, he is in for a rough time. Half the time he cannot even get interviewed because he has no way of knowing when his name is called. He cannot hope to get much help from want ads in the paper, either, because the words "An Equal Opportunity Employer," in the ads refer to race, creed or color, and far too many employers stop there. The words "equal opportunity" should include the handicapped, and perhaps the day will come when they will.

As I look back on what I have said, I am acutely aware that it may seem that nothing has ever been done for the deaf. We know this is not so. We wish to recognize the many positive things that have been accomplished by the Department. We believe that for every negative item there can be found one that is positive. I was much encouraged yesterday by the announcement that this conference will lead to implementation. We are tired of talking about these things and think it is time we stop talking and do something!

Potentials for Employment of the Deaf at Levels in Keeping with Their Intellectual Capabilities

Delivered in 1972.

At a time like this I have some very irresistible temptations to make some very profound statement. And the first of these is that deaf people can do anything that hearing people can do . . . except hear. The second one of these is that ears are cheap. It's what's between the ears that counts.

As a keynote speaker, I am aware that I should be saying enough about the Potentials for Employment of Deaf People at Levels in Keeping with Their Intellectual Capabiltiies to turn you on—but not so much that I will instead turn you off. With that in mind, and to emphasize what I have already said about the abilities of deaf people, let me stress some points.

One of them is that an employer is no big-hearted angel. He expects his employees to earn their keep, and this is especially true of his deaf employees. But the road to employment for a deaf person is filled with pitfalls. First is that when a deaf person seeks employment, he runs into a "No" concept. Personnel staff have never run into a deaf person before. Until this moment, "Deaf" has only been a word in their vocabulary and when faced with reality, the response is generally negative.

The first thought that arises is: "How will we communicate?" Then they think of how communication will take place on the job. And after that, all the possible hazards that a person who can't hear will be exposed to. Finally, they consider the language problems and conclude there is no place in their organization for deaf people. Of course, if a company has had prior experience with deaf employees, it is a different ball game— one which could be better—or worse—than what I have described. If the previous experience has been good, then more deaf people in the labor force are welcomed. If it has been bad, "no deaf people need apply." We have not yet reached the point where we, deaf people, are recognized as individuals.

But what of the negatives? In the first place, communication is simple. Depending upon the education of the deaf person and the position for which he is being considered, communication can be with pencil and paper, which is a novel idea in a country where education is compulsory. If necessary, there are many other ways to communicate. Sometimes the deaf person can even read lips. Much of the communication problem exists largely in ones mind. We have often been challenged about the use of the telephone. This is generally seen as a barrier for middle manage-

85

ment positions and above. But as practice has shown, most mid-level executives have secretaries who not only can answer the phone and interpret the call, but also serve as interpreters at staff meetings and other public contacts. We do this every day at the NAD, and it works very well.

The second issue is safety. The most frequent concerns relate to factories: What about overhead cranes? How will a deaf person know they are moving? How can one tell when machines break down? You can't hear these things, so you won't know. Well, most deaf people have been deaf for a long time. They may be deaf, but they are not stupid. We (I include myself) know we can't hear. All our lives we have had to be alert to danger, and it is second nature to us now. Overhead cranes are not the only things in life that move, and all machines are not in factories. We are not about to commit suicide. Those of us who were not sufficiently alert are already dead or crippled, hit by cars that we did not see. When a machine breaks down, I can feel it. In a noisy environment, the ability to sense a malfunction is often superior to the ability to hear one.

Another point that needs to be made is that more often than not deafness is an asset rather than a handicap. The deaf worker cannot work and talk at the same time. Consequently, he concentrates on what he is doing, which makes for greater safety (and productivity) than one would get from a worker who can work while talking to co-workers. In some situations the results can be surprising. During World War II, I had a great deal of difficulty in getting a job as a machineshop inspector. The personnel people were aghast at the idea. "But-but-but," they said, "you will not be able to talk with the machinists." Which was not quite true, because I could talk with them—they couldn't talk with me. That is a significant difference. I got the job. I also changed the area in which I worked to the most productive in the plant, because operations were on a piece-work basis; that is, the more parts a machinist produced, the higher his pay. When an inspector rejected a part the machine had to shut down for adjustment. This led to arguments between the machinists and the inspectors, with attendant delays. How do you argue with a deaf inspector? Inspectors are like baseball umpires—they seldon change their stance. Arguing only wastes time. Since arguing with a deaf person was obviously futile, the machines shut down faster for me, adjustments were quicker, and productivity was higher.

The expectations of employers most often produce the barriers that impede employment of deaf people at their true potential. One young lady came to my office for help. She was frustrated because: "When I apply for a job I am usually asked, 'Can you read my lips?' and when I say 'No', the boss loses interest." So I told her, "The next time you are asked that question, say 'Yes, if you speak plain.'" Well, she has a job now. She still doesn't read lips, but now her boss thinks it is *his* fault!

As I have said, the barriers that restrict employment are largely imaginary. The determining factor is the skills deaf people have. I manage a business now—a complex business—and like everyone at this administrative level, as well as those at mid-level, I have a secretary. One can teach ones secretary to sign and to serve as a personal interpreter. When I go to meetings, she goes with me. It doesn't cost much, because generally she wouldn't have much to do, if I weren't in the office, anyway. This obviously would apply to everyone. I know of deaf persons in occupations that you would consider incredible: A deaf medical doctor, a deaf college professor whose students hear, deaf insurance agents whose clients are not related to deafness, just to name a few. Once we get people accustomed to the idea that a deaf person is a human being whose only difference is the inability to hear, we will get some place. Deaf people can work. They have good hands, good minds, good abilities, and will use them if given the opportunity.

Too often problems arise because employers do not realize that deaf workers are human beings. They give us jobs and keep us in those jobs, simply because they do not know what else to do with us. Then they wonder why the deaf employee is dissatisfied. All humans—including deaf ones—desire recognition and the opportunity to use their skills at the highest level possible.

All we ask for is a chance. Given such a chance the benefits are considerable. Because such opportunities are rare, you get an employee who is loyal and who will remain in your employ as long as you will have him.

You can create imaginary problems that do not really exist. I had this problem in computer training. I had one woman who was working her way up from the bottom. She started working as a keypunch operator. And apparently succeeding. The company was selfishly interested in allowing her to work her way up, then she came to the level where she was preparing to study programming. Her immediate supervisor turned her down. The question, of course, was, "Why?"

"Because she can't hear."

I later said, "But the computer can't talk."

That, I think, is the way to approach the problem. The deaf individual has a lot of talent, a lot of things to offer to industry—if you accept him and use him wisely.

Building Local and State Community Organizations

Reprinted from Planning for Deaf Community Development, *New York: New York University Deafness Research & Training Center, 1972.*

I think I would like this morning to begin by expounding the Ketchup Bottle Law, and, perhaps, after I have thoroughly confused you, begin to make some sense.

Everyone who has ever tried to get ketchup out of a bottle knows how difficult it is. Obviously, if it were as hard to get the ketchup in the bottle as it is to get it out, there would be no law because ketchup manufacturers would have gone broke long before this. In essence, then, the Ketchup Bottle Law means it is easy to get in but hard to get out. And this is an immutable law which can readily be explained.

For example, it is easy to get in bed at night and hard to get out in the morning. Or take a look at this hotel. There are exit signs everywhere. But where do you see a sign that says "Entrance?" Architects are no fools. They know that getting in is easy. Getting out is when people need help and hence the "Exit" signs. Or take marriage. When two young people decide to get married, it's very easy. Everybody jumps in to help make things go smoothly. Once you are in, try wiggling out! Or take government. Our government found it easy to get into the war in Viet Nam and has been trying to get out ever since.

What I am trying to say is that since it is so easy to get into a situation and so hard to get out, one should approach a new idea with caution. Look at us: 100 years ago someone had the idea he could make "hearing" people out of us and we are still trying to get out of that!

Organizational Structure for Voluntary Organization

An effective organization, whether it be a state association, a club, or whatever, must observe some fundamental rules. Some of these are well known and I will touch on them only briefly.

There must be a clearly defined objective or objectives. It does not matter especially what these objectives are so long as you know what they are. For example, if you are in a social club and the objectives of the club are social, that's all right. The purposes of the organization are usually contained in the bylaws and the bylaws should be changed if the objectives change.

With the objectives already stated, the quest for membership begins. Since organizations are formed for reasons of common interests or needs, the task is to make sure your members and/or potential members understand the purposes of the organization and how or what such an organization can do to meet these purposes. More often than not, the failure to attract members stems from one of two causes:

(1) There has been no general and persistent attempt to get new members; and

(2) The potential members do not understand how membership might benefit them, either as an individual or a community or both.

Administration of the organization must follow the rules set down by the bylaws and supplemented by whatever directions are provided by the membership. Too often, something is decided upon by the members which turns out to be impossible to do. When this happens, there is a tendency to ignore the directive, which, in turn, causes a loss of confidence in the officers and the organization as well. Additionally, because of the nature of the organization, it often happens that persons elected to office are not completely aware of the objectives of the group, and, when they are, have no idea of how to carry out their responsibilities.

My purpose is to offer some suggestions as to how to overcome the weaknesses that now exist. While I have chosen the State Association as a model, much of what I would like to suggest is equally applicable to clubs, if allowances are made for things that a club might not be able to get.

Going back, most organizations already have bylaws and there are usually provisions to change or amend the existing rules if need be. The important thing is to note that the rules or bylaws must be followed. When it is not possible to obey the bylaws, then they should be amended legally to reflect the wishes of the membership. Under no circumstances can the laws be ignored or decisions of the membership voided. All that happens is to develop a loss of faith and a loss of interest in the organization. It is always possible to ask for amendments and/or reconsideration of a motion. The only real problem is to be sure that when asking for reconsideration that this be done not because you don't agree with the decision, but because of the factors. The integrity of the organization is essential to its success. It must be recognized that the majority rules. This is not to say that the majority is always right, but right or wrong, it rules. It is the responsibility of the organization's leaders to provide guidance and leadership so that the members will go along. This is usually possible, but whenever it turns out that it isn't then the wishes of the members must be followed.

The leaders, of course, must have a clear idea of the objectives of the association. While these are stated in the bylaws, they are usually broadly stated, so that some interpretation is required. What I am saying is that each idea or course of action must be matched to an objective, so that if you are undertaking some project you know why and how the project will help your goal. Let us use the National Census for the Deaf as an example. The objective here is to gather information that will improve educational and employment opportunities for people who are deaf by determining the number of children who will be needing schooling in the near future; discovering the kinds of employment now open to adults and the number of persons needing or who might need the services of rehabilitation or other social service agencies. It is not always easy to see the connection between the proposal and the objective, especially since there are times when there isn't one. But, generally, it is possible to determine this relationship. In other instances needs can be identified, and one must think how these needs can be met. I will come back to this shortly.

Now, membership. Obviously, to be effective and to meet the objectives of your bylaws, you will need money. While it would be unrealistic to suggest that the entire sum needed for effective operation can be raised from within the deaf community, it is necessary that membership be increased. Few associations put on sustained or regular membership drives and even fewer seek to enroll the families of their members. But by regular efforts to build up membership; by repeated efforts to build up membership; by repeated efforts to let potential members know what you are doing and what you have done, membership will grow. Brochures can be used for this, news releases, perhaps to your club papers, and your school papers can help. You need to state what you have done, or what has been done, and your role in doing this, as well as how this will help your members or the people in your state.

In this respect, and with respect to preparing proposals to meet the needs of your members, it is recognized that on the state level, one does not have the time or money to do all this, which is correct. But, what is overlooked is your resources in the NAD. The NAD has many things available that could be used to assist in your program. Little of this is being used now. For example, we can supply you with the addresses of local papers; we could, if asked, prepare brochures on membership that can be personalized yet used by all states for recruitment; we can supply your members' addresses on pressure sensitive labels, and, if need be, assist with mailing. While it would undoubtedly cost something for this, the cost would be relatively small. We can, if the States would do their part, provide all kinds of information regarding services to the deaf. Information could be supplied relative to all the existing and proposed laws, all the clubs, club publications, special programs in all the states.

This information is valuable in several ways. First, it might suggest solutions to some of your problems. Then again, the fact that a law exists in one or more states can be a strong point in securing similar laws in your state. What is needed here is a systematic gathering of information, and regular transmittal to the NAD Home Office. It is probably true that our Research Department might do well to devise a form indicating data to be collected to ease the load on the State Officers. I note that the chairman of our Research and Development Committee is present, and hope he is listening. Knowing what exists elsewhere can be of great help.

Another area is in professional help. While the NAD does not have too many professional staff members, we have a few. We also have a long list of consultants who are available to assist an association in developing proposals for consideration by State Agencies, both public and private. This is to say, if a state needs help with its educational program, we can and will provide prominent educators to assist in telling the state what and why. The same thing is true in rehabilitation, and in areas of community service. We can provide assistance in writing proposals, news releases, applications for support; pretty near anything one might think of. But we cannot do this unless requested. We must have enough feedback and basic information on which to base our help. This is because conditions vary from state to state, and only the people on the scene will know what their needs are.

There are many fundamental things that are applicable to all states. One, for example is voter registration. If you have not heard about this already, you will. This is an election year. Do you know how many of your members are registered voters? Are you doing anything to increase the number who are registered? Again, while we do not have one, it is possible for the NAD to design a basic brochure that could be used by *all* states explaining why it is important to register and vote, and the states can add individually, where and how to register. We can arrange for the use of voting machines so that your members can learn how to use them. While all of these things cost money, by printing brochures in quantity, the cost of each will be much less than if we print only 5000. The same thing is true of membership brochures and other material that the states might need or want.

There are other things that might be done. Probably one of the simplest is getting "visibility" so that people can find out that you exist. One way to do this is via the telephone book. If you have any people on your board who have telephones, that phone should be listed in the name of your organization. I am not sure if it would also be possible to list the correct address as in the case of a club, but that is not the main idea. The main idea is that if people have any need to contact someone relating to deafness, they can find some source. Persons moving into the city who have deaf children, for example, could find you. So could people who may have deaf neighbors, or people who became deaf recently; even employers and prospective employees. It could very well be that no one will be available to answer the phone, but the listing also provides an address so that when one fails to get an answer by phone, he or she can write or come to the address listed.

Another effort might be to seek to establish outreach services within or in conjunction with local organizations. We need many kinds of services for our members and prospective members. If these services could be provided, it would strengthen the organization. How about trying to get rehabilitation counselors to operate out of clubs? If this could be done, the rent the State pays could help provide better clubrooms or a better location for the club. Also services for the elderly. Clubs may not see these services as part of their objectives, and they may very well not be. But the provisions of such services can do things to strengthen the organization: 1) Increase membership with an attendant increase in income; 2) Increase income through cooperative rental; 3) Increase attendance because when people come for a specific reason they will stay to socialize; 4) Increase involvement because parents and other relatives sometimes accompany the deaf person in need of rehabilitation or other social services. This latter is also important. I believe someone else will discuss this more fully, so I just want to note that involvement with parents and others interested in the problems of the hearing impaired is essential. If they won't come to you, go to them. At this time, it is likely the reason they aren't coming to you is that they don't know you exist. But whatever the reason, get involved!

In essence, then, it seems that the state associations are not making efficient use of their most important resource, the NAD Home Office. As you know, the NAD is run by state associations. The Home Office will do whatever the Council of Representatives decides should be done, assuming, of course, that it can be done. There are many things that could be done, or at least tried, if the states are interested. For example, how about a Credit Union? I do know there are advantages to credit unions, and if the states want it or anything else, we'd try and get it. The NAD meets in Miami in July. It's your move!

Acceptance Speech for Dan Cloud Award

Given at California State University at Northridge, 8 June 1973.

Thank You. Between the time I first learned that I was selected to receive this award and this evening, one thing became perfectly clear: there is no way to accept honors gracefully. One can be a good loser, or a gracious winner, with relative ease. However, where honors are concerned, there is little one can do other than say, "Thank you," which I have done. In this particular instance, I am aware that I have been inducted into real fast company and that it will take some doing to keep up with the previous recipients: Marshall Hester, Edgar Lowell, Boyce Williams, Robert Sanderson, and David Denton. One cannot help but feel humble and proud to be considered worthy of membership in such a select circle and can only hope that he is worthy of inclusion. Actually, if anyone deserves an award, it is my wife, who has displayed remarkable forbearance in the entire—well, I better not say how many—years of our marriage. Without her encouragement and support I guess there would be little I could have done. She is here tonight to share this occasion with me.

We face critical times today. At the moment it appears that we are headed back to the "Dark Ages" and that all the progress we have made in upgrading education and improving services for the deaf over the past decade are to be wiped out—eloquent testimony that it takes years to build but only moments to destroy that which took those years to develop. This is our situation in all parts of the country. Almost all of the federally-supported programs for the deaf have gone under willy-nilly, with no regard to the merits nor effectiveness of what was being cancelled, while those projects that remain have been drastically curtailed so as to be almost ineffectual.

To the best of my knowledge terminated programs include CSUN's Leadership Training Program; Langley Porter's project, under Dr. Schlessinger; the interpreter research work, at Illinois, under Dr. Steve Quigley, and the mental health project, headed by Dr. Altschler, in New York, not to mention support for the R.I.D. and the Census. These are but a few of the major projects that have felt the Nixon-administration ax. There are quite a few others, especially in the area of training.

Despite all this, there may very well be some benefits to be reaped from the ruins. For one thing, it has always been known that if we, in the area of deafness, are to truly serve our people, we must make maximum use of our resources, our manpower and our money. Too often in the past we have fallen into the trap of "easy" money and, in our eagerness to serve, to fill the many gaps that exist for the deaf in education, vocational training, rehabilitation, and community and social services. We have creáted duplicative programs, organizations which, while needed, were incapable of standing alone, and we have permitted ready federal money to blind us to the realities of our existence. One of these realities is best expressed by what I call the Ketchup Bottle Law. In essence the Ketchup Bottle Law is an immutable law of nature based on the fact that it is easier to get into a given situation than it is to get out. This is where we are now. We have gotten into situations from which we will have great difficulties in extricating ourselves. We have put ourselves into the position of giving lip service to all that we profess to believe in, and our goals have largely turned out to be paper.

There were many positive developments over the past decade that we can put to work to turn the tide that is now going against us. I can remember way back in the early sixties when the consumer wasn't king and the futile efforts we made then to insure that deaf people had the right to some self-determination, some input as to the scope and direction of programs affecting our own welfare. It was a radical notion then. In truth, it is a radical notion now.

To be sure, we go through the motions. The professionals profess to desire input from the consumer, and in many cases consumers are invited to meetings, workshops and the like. But are we heard? Perhaps the best answer could be had by pointing to state and national consumer conventions which are notable for the lack of professionals in attendance. If, as it is said, consumer involvement is essential to effective program development, and if it is true that the voice of the deaf must be heard in the halls of the state legislatures, why aren't the professionals on hand when consumers convene? We find this to be the case all over the nation. The consumers meet, but the professionals aren't there to listen. The professionals say that the consumer is the motivating force that must operate to insure that funds are available to meet their needs but they do not often attempt, especially on the state level, to open two-way communication with the people they wish to serve.

Deaf people, or at least some of us, have learned the value of protest. We have learned that we are citizens and we have rights and privileges that are inherent in all citizens of this nation. We have, or at least some of us have, learned that we do not have to accept crumbs from the community table. We do not need to apologize for our handicap nor tremble lest what little we have be taken away from us by the vast and alien world of people who hear.

If we have any difficulty here, it is that there are not enough of us who have gotten the message and are fulfilling our responsibilities. So it may not come as a surprise if I ask those people who are being graduated tomorrow, "Are you prepared to pay for your education?"

Years ago when I was in college I took it for granted that there was a lot of truth in the old adages, particularly the one saying that you have to pay for what you get, often in coin other than cash. It never occurred to me that anyone felt otherwise nor that there was any doubt that the coin demanded of college-trained deaf persons was and is service.

It is explicit in our society that the strong aid the weak, the rich are compelled to aid the poor, and college graduates must help those who, through lack of opportunity or ability, have not gained the knowledge necessary to assume leadership in their communities. It seems to me that this is your challenge. Whatever profession you are to follow, even though it be remote from the traditional fields of service to your peers, you have this responsibility: the responsibility of using your knowledge, your skills, and your training for the betterment of the people in your community.

The responsibilities of community leadership are heavy and often irksome. This creates a tendency, as we have noted in the NAD, to "let George do it", from which we have derived our "Order of Georges". But it is safe to say that, today, George is busy, and if we are going to do what needs to be done, we will have to do it.

The events of the past decade, and especially of the more recent years, have thoroughly dispelled the notion that as a minor minority we are helpless pawns in the larger scheme of things. We have shown that with determination and cooperation we can change the course of events to take our needs and desires into consideration. We have proven that working together with people who have common interests, we can reach out and overcome the obstacles that face us today.

It is up to you and others like you to demand—not only of your government but also of your professionals, teachers, counselors, social workers, interpreters or whatever—viable plans that will provide the kind of services deaf people need and are entitled to. We cannot afford the luxury of ego trips, of dissipated energy, and the frittering away of our resources. We cannot afford to continue on the basis that each man is an island complete unto himself and each can succeed by going his own way.

We must somehow come up with a set of priorities and a means of coordinating the efforts of people in the field to achieve these priorities. Professionals are guilty, I believe, of nothing worse than a desire to help, a desire that is so strong and compelling that it leads them to forget that they are not alone and that what they do must be shared with others, if it is to be truly meaningful. At the moment, for example, I believe there are five summer interpreter training programs scheduled in various parts of the country. That's great! We probably could use ten such programs, but so far as I know, none are sharing their efforts with the Registry of Interpreters for the Deaf or with each other. Yet, to be effective, it is essential that pluses and minuses be shared, that all might benefit from the positive aspects of each program and all might avoid or minimize that which is found to be negative. In the final analysis, the people who stand to gain or lose are not the institutions that will conduct the programs, nor even the students who will take the courses, although if the program they enroll in is not the best, they are being cheated. We are the people who suffer from the failure to share experiences. We are the people who are deprived of the services we need to insure we can maintain ourselves as independent members of society.

Since we, as deaf people, are the ones who are most affected by what happens, we must make our feelings known and insist that our institutions, organizations, and training programs explore all ways by which they can not just function but be of maximum service under the circumstances. It is for us to say, "It is not what you want, but what is best for the deaf that must be the determining factor." And once that factor is known, we, as deaf people, must not sit idle while these same institutions battle—not for their survival, but for ours.

The ultimate responsibility for what will happen to us now and in the future lies in our own hands. It is ironic to think that as a minor minority we are theoretically small enough to be an extremely potent political force—a force that could be far more effective and dramatic than that mustered by the larger minorities which are much too easily split into factions and cliques. The answer to our needs lies in effective leadership. The challenge of leadership is yours. Pray that you are up to it.

Editorial We

Reprinted from Dee Cee Eyes, *June 15, 1974*

Old Editors never die, they just lose their marbles. And to find this old war horse subbing for Will Madsen who is off to the wilds of Alaska just proves it.

We are grateful however for the opportunity to sound off once more especially on a subject which is becoming more and more of an irritant. And that is sign language. Once upon a time sign language belonged to deaf people. It was like the bunny that tried to associate with the antiseptic baby and the prophylactic pup in the sense that it wasn't carbolated and it wasn't sterilized but it belonged to us. And we loved it and cherished it despite all efforts of our all-knowing mentors to convince us that it was a crutch, a liability and a wall that prevented us from becoming "normal" whatever "Normal" was supposed to mean. And for close to 100 years we have resisted all efforts to make us into something we are not and never wanted to be in the first place. Then suddenly Sign Language was "IN." It is the thing today decorated with cherries and whipped cream and now we call it "total communication." Of course, we are glad that finally after all these years of frustration and dogged determination to keep what was ours we have achieved recognition. We have overcome to the extent that education finally has come to grips with the problem and agreed that we, the deaf people, were right after all.

If that were the end of the matter, it would be great. And as in the fairy tales, we could all "live happily ever after." But that isn't all. With the acceptance of signs, everybody got on the bandwagon. So many people got on this bandwagon that there suddenly were too many and some had to be pushed off and guess who the some were? The deaf, of course. Now everybody is in the business of improving sign language, everybody knows more about it than the poeple who have been using it for a hundred years and more. It was bad enough when we found that every Tom, Dick and Harry was inventing signs for words without regard for the deaf community and for that matter without regard for each other, but it became the height of the ridiculous when they began to "improve" on signs that were already in existence. It seems high time that the deaf community ought to get up in arms and suggest politely or not so politely, if you wish, that this is our language. We can and do appreciate help in speeding its growth, but leave what we have alone. We do not need or want improvements on the signs we already have, and if you want to add or help add to our vocabulary, fine. But where does the deaf community fit into this project? Like it or not, you can invent every kind of sign imaginable but they are only as good as the people who use them. If we are to use them, then we must approve of them, and in some cases it seems we do, but in the long run it should be noted that we are not even asked, and by and by the worm will turn.

The Ketchup Bottle Law

Speech at the Margaret Sterck School, Wilmington, Delaware, 7 May 1975.

Thank you. As I stand here this evening, I am reminded of the discovery of a new law of nature. It is called the Ketchup Bottle Law. Most of you are familiar with Ketchup bottles and are aware that if it were as difficult to get Ketchup into a bottle as it is to get it out, manufacturers would have gone broke long ago. This law is immutable. For example, it is easier to get into bed at night than to get out of it in the morning. You can see, throughout this building, clearly marked "EXIT" signs. But where do you see a sign that says "ENTRANCE?" That's because architects are no fools. They know there is no problem getting into a building. It's when you try to get out that you need help.

How about matrimony? When one decides to go into wedlock, the whole world acts to make this as easy as possible. But once you are in—try getting out! Other examples might be governmental policies. Look at Viet Nam. It was easy to get into that war, but where are we now?

Actually, when one gets an idea and adopts a given concept, if it is a good one, that usually works pretty well. But when it is decided that change is needed, then trouble begins. This, of course, is the basis for the Ketchup Bottle Law.

It is also the basis for my talk this evening. We have a new school here in Delaware. It is one that has not yet been involved in a larger number of situations that require change. And I believe that extreme care should be taken not to get into these situations, because by the immutable Law of the Ketchup Bottle, once you get in, you'll have trouble getting out. The Ketchup Bottle also may help explain some of our problems today. We have had educational systems and theories that date back over 100 years. Many of these have been controversial, it is true. Still whatever system we developed is in the bottle, and it is difficult to shake it loose. I do not believe that there is any way one can keep out of a Ketchup bottle. Decisions have to be made. Courses of action have to be planned. The only thing one can do is to try to plan as carefully as possible and as thoroughly as possible so that there will be a long period of time before one has to try to get your Ketchup out of its bottle.

With respect to education, in general, and education of the deaf, in particular, there are a number of key words that need emphasizing. They are: relevance, involvement, and accountability. Three little words. I seem to recall there was a song by that title once. If you don't remember it, perhaps I am older than I thought. In any case, the first of these words is probably the most important. Education is supposed to mean something. Just this morning I read that the development of whatever speech a child might have is of primary importance, but that our concern as a school, should be broader than speech development alone: our responsibility is to try to bring the child to that point of communication which, in turn, leads him to the threshold of learning, especially that of language learning . . ." There is more to report, of course, but I have seized this part for two reasons. First, because while the development of speech is of great importance, it is not, or should not be, the primary goal in the education of a deaf child. It also illustrates the kind of thinking that has prevailed for over 100 years. Deaf people submit, nay, we insist that the primary goal of a school is to educate. Deaf children need, more than anything else, the knowledge of the world around them so that they can successfully maintain their place in society when they are adults. Children also need the language skills by which they can express their thoughts and emotions. They need communiation. Communication with their parents, siblings, friends and the world around them. The mistake we have been making all these years is interchanging speech and communication. If speech were communication, why do we have our generation gap? Why is there so little communication between parents and teenagers? Between colleges and their students? All have speech, but no communication.

Because we have been so concerned with this, we have failed, really, to provide the kind of education the deaf child needs. This is where *relevance* comes in. If there is to be an educational program at all, it must have a goal. It must be geared to the ultimate needs of the individual, and not to what we might like to have. To my knowledge, this has never been done. For the most part, educational programs for the deaf have been geared to the needs of hearing children. There have been modifications here and there, to be sure, but basically the program is that designed for hearing children.

The second word is *involvement.* Are deaf people involved in education of the deaf? For many generations there has been a quotation with which you are all familiar. It is, "You can lead a horse to water, but you can't make him drink," which is another way of saying that no matter how good your program may be, if it is not what we need or want, it won't succeed. I am disturbed by the fact that all the educational research is done with children. It would be more difficult to do this with adults, to be sure. Still, if the purpose of education is to prepare children for adulthood and their place in society, then more research needs to be done with the adults. This will not only determine the effectiveness of the present educational program but also indicate those areas where our needs are not being met. Only in this way can one devise a system that will be effective. Further, deafness is an insidious problem. It is so foreign to nature—or perhaps I should say to the auditory world—that the little things that have so much bearing on a deaf person's life are overlooked. Even the professionals, who are both trained and dedicated, have been known to miss these little but critical things. For example, the White House Conference on Aging had provision for the handicapped. They had provisions for the blind, the wheelchair cases, but nothing for the hearing impaired. Hearing loss is well recognized as a natural process of aging, and there are at least 600,000 elderly people who suffer from this. But it was forgotten. Or take the dormitories at Gallaudet College. When the men and women's residence halls were built, there were phone jacks in the rooms. There were not visible signals by which a person could know someone was at the door, however; no visible alarm system to alert the occupants in case of fire. Things like this can be avoided by involving deaf people in the planning of programs. I am especially reminded of a film made by the American Red Cross, especially for deaf children, on water safety or swimming. The Red Cross director was proud of his work, and rightly so. He had made a real effort to be of service to the deaf child. He has consulted with a parents' group in Georgia in planning this film and was taken aback when I asked, "Is it captioned?" It wasn't. A more personal reason for advocating involvement comes from an incident involving my own daughter. I had asked her to meet a deaf friend who was arriving at Dulles Airport and bring him over to see me. She lives near the airport. For some reason, she arrived a bit late, and failing to see my friend, went to the public address system to have him paged. It wasn't until she heard his name repeated for at least five minutes that she remembered he couldn't hear. My daughter grew up with deaf parents. For most of her life she had been involved in the work I had been doing with the deaf community. She was my ears, my interpreter, my telephone voice when needed. If anyone could be expected to remember that deaf people can't hear, I guess she qualified. Yet she forgot. This is why involvement of the deaf community is so vital to the success of a program. In many cases we can provide positive suggestions for implementation. In all cases, we will be able to relate what is planned to our hearing loss.

Finally, there is *accountability*. If you are very religious, perhaps it is sufficient to leave that between you and God. But to be more pragmatic about it, the educator is accountable to society and particularly to the parents. It is important that parents be given an honest assessment of their children's prospects and potential; that the parents be given all the information possible about their child's future. It is also important that the educator be thoroughly prepared to supply this information.

Teacher training programs do not provide this knowledge. It is not readily found in textbooks, since there is a wide gap between theory and practice in any field. The widest, however, is in the area of deafness. Parents ought to ask their childrens' teachers about deaf adults. Do the teachers know any? Have they ever been to a meeting of deaf people? Are they familiar with the organizations of deaf adults? What do they know about the social and economic attainments of the older deaf person? Children become adults, you know, and while I am aware that my mother still thinks I am her baby, I can assure you, your child, too, will be an adult someday.

In the meantime, your child is a part of your family. He is aware that he has and is giving you problems. While he may not be able to express himself too well on this, you can be assured he knows. He also knows that whatever he is, he can't help it. He doesn't want to be deaf any more than you want him to. So he can only hope you will accept him for what he is. He hopes you will adjust to him, because he cannot adjust to you. In the adult deaf community, family ties are not too strong. This is because traditionally the effort was to change the child to fit the family, rather than fit the family to the child. As I say this, I realize I am oversimplifying. It is not really possible, nor desirable, to change the family to fit the child. But some accommodation must be made to make him an integral part of the family, lest at some future date you awake to realize how far apart you have grown.

Total Communication—As the Adults See It

Keynote Address to the Convention of the International Association of Parents of the Deaf, Washington, D.C., 1975

I am most happy to have this opportunity to speak today on the subject of "Total Communication." I also would like to take a different approach to this question, because I think more than enough has been written and said about the educational aspects of what this is and what it will or will not do for your children. As you know, the National Association of the Deaf defines Total Communication as "the right of all deaf people to learn to use all forms of communication available to develop language competence." This includes the full spectrum: gestures, speech, formal sign language, fingerspelling, speechreading, reading, writing and making use of any residual hearing through amplification. This is often misinterpreted as to refer only to manual communication probably because all of the other ingredients of the whole picture have always been there. It is only the addition of manual communication to the package that makes it "total."

Let me discuss briefly some of the more persistent myths surrounding the use of manual communicaton and the implications which have been placed on this in connection with the Total Communication picture.

First, of course, is that Total Communication is only sign language, that the adoption of Total Communication will result in the elimination of speech and speechreading once and for all. This is far from true. The deaf population has always believed, and continues to believe, in the need and desirability of speech and speechreading. We believe and endorse auditory training and are among the leaders in suggesting that children should be provided with hearing aids and other means of stimulating amplification. At no time have we ever suggested that any part of the overall "total" aspect of Total Communication be neglected. We do believe, however, that the teaching of speech and speechreading should be only a part of the educational process of the child—not the end-all and be-all of his life. We believe, it must be said, that in the total concept this means that less time will be devoted to the teaching of speech and speechreading and more will be allocated to the purpose for which you send your child to school—to be educated. We do not and never have believed that being able to speak constitutes an education or can be an adequate substitute for one. The purpose of school is to provide an education. The purpose of education is to enable one to get along in the world. That means to be able to make a living, to enjoy the benefits of society, and to enjoy the fruits of ones labor. It does not mean anything else. It should not mean anything else. Speaking as an adult, there is no point that I can see in being paid $35,000 a year if one cannot enjoy it, does not know what to do with it. Nor is there any point in associating socially with anyone unless you enjoy their company and are fully and freely able to take part in social interaction which is what you are talking about in the first place. What good is it to be among people who hear if you are isolated? What pride can one have in being friends with people who are only sorry for you? And what satisfaction can one get from knowing that he has climbed the highest mountain only to find that the result is no better or greater than if he had never even started?

Most of all, how can a deaf person progress without the constant reinforcement which he needs and cannot get by any other method? You have experienced a little the problems related to having a deaf child. You know already that your deaf child does not, cannot learn by the same methods that come so readily to children who hear. You are aware that hearing children develop language effortlessly. They hear it and in a relatively short time it becomes a second nature to them. No fuss, no muss, no study, no nothing, unless it is prying them loose from the television set at bedtime. On the contrary, every word your deaf child learns he has to be taught. It is a slow and painful process and, even with Total Communication, this process will not, cannot, hope to approximate the ease with which other children learn. This is not because of deafness per se, it is a simple physical fact that one hears more than one sees. You can hear a person in the next room even though you cannot see him. And in hearing him you are getting continual input that never ceases, so that the child who hears is learning every minute that he is awake even if you are just talking on the telephone with your neighbor. Your deaf child, on the other hand, only learns when you are talking to him. If you are not communicating directly to him, he is not learning. If he is playing with his toys, he is not learning language, although he may be learning something else. Unless he has a constant and steady input he does not get all of the things that he needs to know.

Education is more than what is taught in school. Most children learn more outside of school than they do in it. They learn most everything, I think, from their parents and their siblings. I am not sure just how clear this is but it was brought forcibly to mind when I was first married. At that time, my wife asked me to empty the garbage and I was vehement in my refusal. After a time I did some self examination, because I couldn't quite understand why I had reacted so violently. After all, I had no particular objection to this; I wasn't that lazy. And eventually it dawned on me that the reason I refused was that my father never emptied the garbage. And further reflection made it clear that many of the things that I do, say, feel, even eat, have been handed down to me by my family. I should note at this point, if you do not already realize it, that I did not become deaf until I was almost seven years old. And that made as good a case for Total Communication as any I can think of. Children who hear pick up a lot from overhearing conversations not intended for them. They

103

learn to develop social maturity from such unlikely sources as the movies or television, and they shape their behavior on a combination of these. In some families it is considered quite proper for the head of the household to belt his wife around, to show her who wears the pants in the family. And it should not surprise anyone if this habit carries over to second and even third-generation Americans, because that is the way it is done in that family. In one deaf family I know the deaf parents were having all kinds of trouble with their hearing children, because the father was insisting that his teenage daughters go to bed at 9:30. When he was their age that's what he had to do. And he meant well. He was determined that he would see that his children were brought up correctly, even if it killed them and him.

Such an attitude is general today. Many parents of children who are deaf are doing things that defy reason. Sometimes I think I might safely say that they border on insanity. It is one reason why I keep on saying children who are deaf rather than deaf children. This smacks of semantics to many and is not quite understood by others, but it is a vain and perhaps futile protest against the treatment to which such children are subject. At one time not too long ago, I read an article on acupuncture in the Washington Post. In brief, a mother of a four-year-old child was quoted as saying that her son was undergoing treatment for nerve deafness. She thought he was improving although his audiogram did not show it. She also said that the treatments were very painful, and it took two adults to hold the little boy down for the purpose. And I wondered, would any mother do this to a nondeaf little boy? Would any parent subject any child to the agony that required two adults to hold him without any better evidence than that she "thought" he was improving? I did not think so. I do not think you would do this, even though I recognize that hope springs eternal in the human breast and it is not unusual for parents to go hunting high and low for the miracle of miracles that will enable their child to hear. I do not condemn that: I can understand it. But I do not believe that one should completely disregard the feelings of the child who is being "normalized." I guess you might say that there are times when the disease is less troublesome than the cure.

But what has this to do with Total Communication, you ask? Well, if my personal experiences are any basis for discussion, it is because many of you are resisting the evidence of your own senses, your own feelings, because someone told you that to give in, to take the easy way, to be able to talk with your own child would not be good for him. Because you are convinced that only by making him miserable can you hope to lead him to the Garden of Eden and that miracle of miracles called "normalcy." Well, it ain't so! As far as I know, and I have been living with my own deafness for over forty years, there is no substitute for being able to hear. At the same time, not being able to hear is not the greatest catastrophe in the world. What makes it the greatest catastrophe is what is done to the children who are so afflicted, more often than not by people who sincerely want only the best for their child, those who pour out all of their love and all of their lives in the wrong direction on the mistaken assumption that what they are doing is for the child's good. And all of the heartbreak, all of the frustration, all of the anguish that you experience will fade away on the day your child speaks fluently and takes his rightful place in society.

Unfortunately, what is overlooked in this process is that the child is denied all that makes life worth living. He is cut off from his parents and is unable to learn or understand all of the things that make life worth living. It is not without reason that research shows that the deaf person is socially immature, suspicious, and somewhat paranoid in nature. Why shouldn't he be? The things that other children learn in family situations have been denied to us. The inter- and intrapersonal relations that make for a socially stable and mature individual are mysteries as far as we are concerned, because we have never had the opportunity of overhearing as have our hearing siblings how specific situations are handled. Why is it that I got hell for messing up my room, but my brother can get away with it? Why do I get clobbered when I lie, but my sister lies like crazy and nobody does anything about it? How does one go about saying, "I'm sorry," when he never heard it said before in any situation anyhow? Why are hearing people so different from people who are deaf? All of these and many more come from informal learning. No one actually teaches one how to say "I'm sorry", nor when such a statement is called for. At the same time, this is not something that is intuitive. It only seems as if it should be, but it is the product of one's environment—an environment which the child who is deaf does not have, unless it is a Total Communication one.

Your child who is deaf needs the opportunity for this kind of casual learning. He needs to be able to oversee what his brothers and sisters overhear. He needs even more than that, because, as I said, it is not possible to see as much as one can hear. He also needs time to be a child, not an object that is to be taught all the time. He needs the time and the opportunity to do things at which he can excel, to build up his ego and his confidence in his ability, and to let him know he is an equal partner in the family. This is perhaps the hardest aspect of it all, because when one talks about "total," that means *all*, and *all* means all the time, not just when your deaf child happens to be watching. In many cases this has not happened and the expected miracles that were to come from Total Communication do not materialize. Often this stems from the failure of the family to remember the fact that in adopting Total Communication it has to be done all the time and preferably by all the members of the family, although I would hesitate to force anyone to adopt a position against his will. Too many fathers are apt to leave the burden of communicating with the child to the mother and sometimes to his brothers and sisters because they, the fathers, are "too busy" to learn to use sign language. You will note that I am reduced as is everyone else to saying sign language when I mean Total Communication. That is because I have to assume that persons who hear will talk. I must also assume that insofar as is practicable your child is already fitted for hearing aids and the only additional component is the use of signs. When this happens, the father is reduced to the status of a maiden aunt asking any who can to "tell him that I love him" and if he don't believe it, WEL-L-L-L.

By the same token, even those who do practice Total Communication as a family are prone to do so only when the sibling who is deaf is present. That is a mistake, both because the constant use of manual communication helps develop proficiency in it and also because it indicates to the child who is deaf that he is not being singled out, that this is normal for his family and he is part and parcel of the whole. But the world does not sign, you say. And so it doesn't depending on which world you are talking about. In my book there are many worlds. There is the world of work, the world at large, the geographic world, and the world that means the most to a child—his family. From his family his horizons may expand to a world that will include his peers and, by and by, it will open up still further to include the children with whom he goes to school, and so on, growing larger as one grows older. But for now you are his world. You are what makes the sun rise and set; you are what he wants to be. It is your love and your approval that he wants the most. The rest of the world can go hang.

But what about later? What happens when he grows up? This is where and why I am here today. I speak for most of the 450,000 deaf adults in this country. I can tell you that despite the fact that the world hears, we get along very well. We do not worry so much about how well we speak but how well we have been educated. We are more concerned that we are not really ready or well-prepared to be well-adjusted members of society, that we do not know enough about the world around us so that we can fit into society and can aspire to higher and better things in life. Most of us recognize that our inability to speak fluently has been a hindrance in getting ahead. We also feel that this hindrance is not so much because we do not speak that well as it is because the public has been led to believe that if we cannot speak fluently, something is lacking, although even the most charitiable estimates say that only one in four children who are born deaf can be taught to speak intelligibly. We also believe that another reason why we do not do so well is that too much time has been expanded on speech and not enough on language and education. We wish to emphasize that language is not speech. Speech may be used to convey language, but there is a basic difference between the two.

As adults we also note that without constant assistance we have difficulty in maintaining what speech we have acquired. In school, with constant practice and skilled teachers, we are able to tackle this task and have some hope of success. But what happens when we leave school? Few of us can afford speech therapists—even fewer have the time after the demands of employment and our families are met even to consider seeking assistance from such sources, and even fewer find the cost worth the results. Most of us do, however, use our speech, if we have any, and many of us who can speak intelligibly find it physically impossible not to speak, even though we also use other means of communication. Sometimes we use both simultaneously as I am doing now, one supporting the other. But I can assure you that, even though I know that as soon as I open my mouth with anyone I will be forced to lipread, I am incapable of not talking, although I do try to use paper and pencil from time to time.

I would also note that my secretary has an eight-year-old deaf son. He is a Total Communication child and his idea of having a private conversation with his mother when I am present is to talk to her without using sign language. He is comfortable in both modes, and most research has already shown that if anything, children who use Total Communication suffer no loss in their ability to speak or read lips. More often than not they do better than those who do not sign, because they have developed language faster, are more assured of their place in their families, and thus more assertive than the child who has not had these advantages.

I am reminded of the story about the little boy who was considered deaf because he never spoke. He, like many of your children, had been hauled from pillar to post and from doctor to doctor seeking some kind of cure for his deafness. The doctors, on the other hand, kept insisting that there was nothing wrong with the boy and in time he would talk. This went on for a number of years until one evening the family was entertaining some distinguished visitors from abroad at a dinner party in which the little boy was included. Suddenly, in the midst of the main course, the little boy said, "These potatoes have lumps in them."

"He can talk! He can talk!" his mother exclaimed. "It is a miracle."

And the boy said, "What are you talking about? Of course I can talk! I always could talk. Why are you making such a fuss about it?"

"Well," said his mother, "if you always could talk, why didn't you do it before?"

"I never had anything to say before."

And that is a moral in itself. If you expect your child to develop speech and to do all of the things that speech is supposed to do, you have to give him the opportunity to have something to say.

Projects, Successes and Activities of the NAD

Address to the Seniors majoring in Deaf Education at Gallaudet College, April, 1974.

If I may, I would like to ramble a little—while assuring you that I will not lose sight of the reason I am here—to show what the NAD does and has done and why it deserves your support.

My personal NAD story starts in 1942 when I was a Senior at Gallaudet. When the NAD started its "Victory Drive" then, that was the first time that I ever heard of the NAD. I did not know who the officers were or even what it did. All I knew was that a national organization for the deaf, or better still, *of* the deaf was a needed thing. All handicapped and minority groups have them. We have the American Foundation for the Blind, The National Association for Advancement of Colored People, Congress on Racial Equality, American Association of Retired People, to name just a few. It seems to me that the smaller the group, the greater the need for a national organization. Please note this was in 1942. Today, I am convinced more than ever that this is true. I am also convinced that it is your job to tell this story—to go out and work on those people who are not now members and explain why they should be. It has always amazed me knowing that the NAD and its member organizations, the State Associations, had to be "sold" to the deaf community. But since it must, I can only note that, in reality, the only way this can be done is for you to do it. I can write this story, but the people who are not now members will never get a chance to read it. You will see them—at work, at play—and you can tell them the score. I really would like to start a fad of some kind that would start, "Are you in the NAD or the State Association?" so that people will have a chance to urge those who are not to join.

Now to discuss why. Why should you or anyone else join the NAD? What does the NAD do to help the deaf? What or how does it affect you as an individual? These are good questions and I will answer them. But before I do, I want to add one more thing and that is—the NAD is its members. If what I do, if my answers do not satisfy you, then you should join and have changes made. The deaf people are the NAD. You are the NAD. And if enough of you think something should be done, it will be done!

O.K., I do not want to go over the whole history of the NAD, so I will start with 1960—with two exceptions which are vitally important to all deaf people. The first occurred in 1890, when the NAD succeeded in opening Civil Service employment to the deaf, and the second is that, since its inception, it has been the sole proponent for what is now called "Total Communication," and the only reason, really, why the U.S. is the only country in the world where deaf teachers of the deaf are accepted. Today, fewer deaf collegians become teachers, but I must say that I have a very strong feeling that were it not for the NAD there would be no Gallaudet College, no NTID, etc. The reason is simple: If Gallaudet graduates were unable to find professional employment, I am sure Congress would have questioned continued support for an institution which turned out overeducated, underemployed alumni. So that is one thing that the NAD did which affects you. If you doubt this, perhaps you would want to explain why there is no college for the deaf in other countries and why Gallaudet-trained deaf people from those countries return to the U.S. after frustrated attempts to crack discrimination barriers in their homeland.

Before I turn to the present, let me say I do not wish to detract from anyones credit. I am aware that only God can do things by Himself. The rest of us must rely on others to help achieve goals. For example, Gallaudet supplied the NAD leaders from 1880 on, in most cases. But I have to focus now on what the NAD did and does. In 1960 the NAD took its present form. Prior to this time I believe most people saw us as a defensive organization, to defend what we had, not to seek more and better programs for the deaf. But in 1960 this began to change, and the NAD itself became more aggressive. I sometimes wonder why we were so backward claiming credit for what we have done. I suppose there were at least three reasons for this:

1. We have a philosophy that says "get things done." It is not important who does it or how it is done, so long as it is done.
2. Others needed the credit.
3. I was personally involved so that any attempt to dispute others claims would look like self interest.

Today, I will make these claims—few can be proved or disproved except by inference. Some can perhaps be supported by individuals who were involved. I do not know, because we just wanted to get things done, not to get into somebody's Hall of Fame. I am fortunate in being involved in this. I have had a "ring-side seat" in history, and I will tell it like it is.

First of all, it was the NAD that opened up the Leadership Training Program to deaf participants. The first program had no deaf people in it, and the NAD went to Dr. Boyce Williams, at Vocational Rehabilitation Administration, and asked why? We wanted to know who wanted "hearing" leaders and why couldn't or shouldn't deaf people be part of the LTP. You know the rest. This is one instance.

Then there is the voice of the deaf in determining their own destiny. Before 1962 or 1963 there was submitted a bill in Congress to establish an interpreter law. That bill was written without consulting deaf people. We raised the question of who proposed this bill and why we (the deaf) had not been asked if we wanted it or not. It did not matter if the bill was good or bad—it was important that the deaf, through their representatives, should be able to say what they needed and wanted. I have a copy of this letter which was printed in DEE CEE EYES, if anyone wants to see it. In addition, at the time that the controversy was raging over the quality of students at Gallaudet, we proposed the establishment of what is now the NTID. I am sure Dr. Elstad and Professor Jonathan Hall will recall this, especially since we had long discussions of a technical institute vs. a high school. But the point I am trying to make is there are no meetings on the deaf today that do not include deaf people, and the NAD helped make this happen.

To go further, the D.C. Association of the Deaf (DCAD) which is now the SBG, is a cooperating member of the NAD. I helped establish it for the express purpose of joining the NAD so whatever was done there was really done by the NAD. One of the main things was the teaching of Sign Language. It has always been a thorn in our sides that teacher training programs for the deaf did not include a course in Sign Language. The NAD has protested this for generations and, when we did in the sixties, the answers were: Where are the textbooks? Where are your curriculum guides? What and how can you teach such a course? Since there wasn't a textbook or a formal program to teach Sign Language, the DCAD developed one. The first Sign Language textbook by Louie Fant was developed in this program. So was Mr. Madsen's *Conversational Sign Language*. Both were tested and modified in the DCAD program. Both were supported by a Federal grant which we had. Subsequent programs in Virginia, Pennsylvania, and Indiana were developed with NAD help. We sent those organizations copies of our grant applications and helped them write theirs. From this grew the Communicative Skills Program and the *A Basic Course in Manual Communication* and the acceptance of Sign Language for credit in countless colleges. Currently, I am told, over 100 colleges that offer some kind of program in deafness—Audiology, Deaf Ed., Vocational Rehab., etc.—also offer Sign Language for credit. There are others as well that do the same, but we have not counted them. In 1962, and I would suspect as late as 1965, there were none—not even, if you can believe it, Gallaudet College, the world's only college for the deaf. I think we can all agree that the National Theatre of the Deaf has done wonders to make Sign Language acceptable. Do you know it was the NAD's Doug Burke who first proposed this? While Doug, as NAD Cultural Chairman, was really aiming for a theatre for the deaf, the idea of a Federally supported program was his.

To continue, we had, as I mentioned, previous interest in interpreter laws. In 1964 there was a workshop on interpreting in Indiana where the RID was born. But from 1964 to 1967 the RID never got moving. It was the NAD that sponsored the 1966 workshop in San Francisco and the NAD that applied for and got the grant that gave the RID a full-time staff and also the ability to save its dues income until now. The NAD also put up 10 percent of the cost of the grant which over a five-year period amounted to at least $50,000.

We have and have had other grants. Contrary to popular belief, these cost the NAD money. We do not make money on them. For 40 or more years people talked about the need to know how many deaf people there are. Everything seemed to depend on that. Do we build more schools? Do the Vocational Rehabilitation services expand? Do the deaf have political clout? While everyone agreed there was a need to know how many people there were, it was the NAD that came out with a proposal to actually do the job, and it cost us a pretty penny. But we needed it and we did it. The results more than justified the cost; these same 40 pre-census years the government has gone by a 1-deaf-person-per-1,000 figure. The census shows this is more than 2.0, so we actually have twice as many people as we were claiming. We also uncovered some interesting educational facts, like few school had any followup program on their school leavers. This meant that they had no idea if their educational programs were good, bad, or just plain lousy. It pointed up the need for follow-up service, because, unless you know what happens to the students you teach, you can't tell how good your school is.

With the census, we also had things like the International Research Seminar on Vocational Rehabilitation of Deaf Persons. This was our bit for our fellow deaf people in other countries and for higher education for the deaf in general. The participants were positively amazed at the deaf people they met and at the fact that in the U.S. we really do run our own show. We are not, as in other countries, window dressing where hearing people actually run everything for the deaf. It was also intended to help stem the flood of oralism that has traditionally been imported from abroad. The 1968 meeting created federal support for next year's World Congress. This we know, will create for all deaf people a better image and for the deaf of America, more prestige. I want to cover the whole ball park, so I will add more quickly. As with the Sign Language programs, we aided in development of State Commissions on the Deaf; we represent the deaf community before Congress, other governmental agencies such as Rehabilitation Services Administration, Bureau of Education for the Handicapped, Civil Service Commission, as well as the Deafness Research and Training Center at New York University, the National Center for Deaf-Blind Youth and Adults, etc. Here we try to speak for the deaf. Many projects that have come out of New York University and the Public Service Department at Gallaudet came from our work. The Civil Service project on discrimination at Gallaudet came from our work. The Civil Service project on discrimination came at our request. Some of the features, in fact the development of the Model State Plan at New York University, was at our request.

Another thing the NAD does is publish books by, for and about the deaf. We sell books, too. We are in this endeavor because we found that where books on deafness existed, they cost so much that nobody would or could buy them. So we became publishers. You might want to note some interesting comparisons—there are dozens of Sign Language books—Watson's, SEE, Riekehof's, to name a few—but those published by the NAD, *Say It With Hands, A Basic Course in Manual Communication* and *Ameslan,* are cheapest. *They Grow in Silence* costs $6.95, while *Deaf People in Professional Employment* is $12.95, published by Charles Thomas, Inc. *Games,* published by the NAD, is $2.00; *Games* by John Joyce Publishers is $12.95. A few days ago I spoke with a chemical engineer from Florida. He said he had visited several libraries in Florida asking for books on deafness. He found two, *In This Sign* by Joanne Greenberg and *They Grow in Silence.* We have also developed some ideas such as the Sign Language playing cards which we will in the future call *Funny Fingers.*

Up to this point I have been talking about general activities. Not mentioned was the fact that the NAD has supported the International Parents of the Deaf ever since it was started. The NAD printed and mailed its first newsletter; we provided rent-free office space, and for one year we paid the salary of its Executive Director. We have provided more financial assistance to the parents than even the Convention of American Instructors of the Deaf to which the IAPD belongs.

Finally, there is the Halex House. While it might be over-emphasized, Halex House is a true symbol. It represents first concrete evidence that deaf people can make major achievements on their own. No one who has ever heard of Halex House can ever say of the deaf community that things must be done for us, because we would be unable to do them ourselves. Halex House also stands for our basic philosophy that "togetherness can pay off." In this building are housed pretty near all the major organizations of and for the deaf. We have the International Parents of the Deaf, the Professional Rehabilitation Workers with the Adult Deaf, the National Association of Hearing and Speech Agencies, and Phonics Inc. Except for religious groups and those that do not maintain offices, only Alexander Graham Bell Association, Convention of American Instructors of the Deaf, Inc., American Speech and Hearing Association, National Fraternal Society of the Deaf, and Registry of Interpreters for the Deaf are not with us. And of these, three, AGB, ASHA and NFSD, have their own buildings. Leaving only the CAID and RID as non-tenants. This togetherness makes for mutual assistance, easy communication and consumer input to all.

Still other efforts come in the area of information and referral. We answer hundreds of letters each week—from children who want to learn to sign or become teachers of the deaf to college students who want to know all about deafness "in 100 words or less," to older people who are losing their hearing or parents who want to know if acupuncture will help. I have a letter here which is only a sample, and I would like to read it to you. I wish I could say we are always successful. We are not. But we try. We find lawyers for deaf people in prison, tangle with insurance companies that will not insure deaf drivers, teacher training programs like that at Clarke and Smith College which offer advanced courses for *hearing* teachers of the deaf. We win some and we lose some, but we are in there pitching. We are active in the local community. The Metro-Wash-

112

ington Association of the Deaf (MWAD) used space in our building for several months until they found a home of their own; the local paper is printed on our press; MSSD students are taught in our offices as part of the Off-Campus Study Program. We take and train rehabilitation clients from Maryland and D.C. Some of our employees were considered unemployable. One was listed as permanently disabled; one was thrown out of the Hot Springs Rehab program for the severely disabled deaf; one was in a mental institution for 30 years.

We also join in Work Study programs in the city. One of our summer workers is now a teacher of the deaf. We got her started. She later came to teach at MSSD. Another stayed with us when she finished high school and helped us start our Sign Language program in Ballou High School, in the District.

As the saying goes, That ain't all! We evaluate films for Media Services and Captioned Films and have provided considerable input to BEH. We also have special arrangements with Bell and Howell whereby we sell movie projectors at very low rates, lower than even other discount houses. We also sell bulbs and other supplies for the projectors. We belong to the United Buyers Service, so that members of the NAD can buy cars for only $100 over cost. We have an auto insurance program with Safeco Insurance Company whereby good deaf drivers who are NAD members are accepted at standard rates. This is good, but we hope to get even better with a true group auto plan. We are aiming for a group auto plan.

We also work with service organizations. The NAD was responsible for the first deaf Lions club in the U.S., and that club sparked the interest of the Lions International in making hearing conservation and deafness a major project. We also have Mrs. Dora Haynes, of Quota International, as a member of the World Federation of the Deaf advisory board. And Quota is now making a major effort in the area of deafness.

I am sure I have missed something. I should mention, for instance, the work we did for the Michigan Association for the Deaf in preparing their grant application for police films, and the time spent trying to help them keep United Fund support. Or the times we testified in Congress in support of Gallaudet's program, the meetings we attend, the speeches we make—all to better the image of all deaf people.

Finally, there are some of our special projects—in particular the Junior NAD and the Cultural Program. Both of these projects are huge undertakings which could and should stand alone. Since I cannot do justice to either of them, let me just mention the highlights of both.

The Junior NAD program is outstanding. While we are still some years away from realizing the full benefit of this effort, the chapters in our schools have given our young people an awareness of the NAD itself; the role that deaf adults can and do play in their communities; the need and responsibilities connected with leadership. Through workshops, seminars and convention, the Junior NAD has been able to bring pupils from different parts of the country together to exchange ideas and information about their schools. The conventions have also enabled many Junior NADers to get some firsthand exposure to institutions, such as Gallaudet College, National Technical Institute of the Deaf, and, we hope in the future, California State University at Northridge, St. Paul Technical Vocational Institute, etc., when or if they are hosts to this convention. This has helped, I am sure, encourage many to continue their education. The involvement with older deaf people has also been stimualting, while the camp program at Swan Lake Lodge has and is an inspiration to everyone. Through this endeavor alone we have been able to interest Lions Clubs and local organizations which had no previous connection with deafness.

The Cultural Program repeats the story. The CP is not as youth-oriented as the Junior NAD, but it has far-reaching effects, and the Miss Deaf America Pageant as well as its aftermath comes close to rivaling the regular Miss America program. Our first Miss Deaf America traveled widely in both programs for the deaf and where deafness was not involved. If we are able to maintain this, there is no doubt that the Cultural Program will have made real strides for all deaf people.

That, I think, is a lot for the $1.50 a year we get. If you have questions, I'll be pleased to answer them if I can. Thank you.

Address to Audiologists

This talk is too potent to be discarded for want of a date. The title is also missing, but the authentic voice that emerges unquestionably belongs to Fred Schreiber. It was probably given in 1975.

When Mr. Purvis invited me to Alabama to speak to you some time ago, I sat down to assess what I knew about audiology and speech pathology, and it may not come as a surprise to most of you that the sum total of my knowledge added up to a little more than zero. At least I can pronounce 'audiology' correctly. However, since I know next to nothing about audiology and not much more than that about speech pathology, it might seem that there is no point to being here at all, and in that case, we might as well all go out for coffee.

Unfortunately, the very fact that I knew so little about audiology is why I am here. There is something very wrong with a situation wherein a profession such as audiology has so little contact with the severely hearing impaired, and the hearing impaired have so little use for audiologists and speech pathologists that their knowledge about both is so minimal. And it stands to reason that something or someone must be responsible for this. As far as I know, the audiologist has considerable contact with the very young, the hearing-impaired child in school, and those people who start losing their hearing later in life. But for the most part, once a deaf or severely hearing-impaired person has left school, he has no further contact with audiology, and not much more, if at all more with speech pathologists. Which is a very sad situation, because it is probable that there are many severely hearing-impaired people in my generation who might benefit from the advances made in hearing aids and testing techniques since the days when we were young.

Considering the importance of hearing, the conservation of hearing, and the undoubted benefits that can accrue from the use of whatever residual hearing a person might have, the audiologist has an extremely important role in the lives of many people. This role involves many aspects of hearing that are not now being attended to. Communication is one area. Obviously it would be very helpful, if not essential, that the audiologist be capable and ready to communicate with his client on the client's terms. Then, inasmuch as it would appear that the same audiologist is perhaps the most appropriate person to provide guidance for parents of young deaf children, he ought to know far more than he does at present about the life style, the capabilities, and the problems of deaf adults, so that he may more adequately advise parents who are concerned with their child's future and provide a more realistic and honest assessment of what the future holds in store. In my opinion, the audiologist should be the person most qualified to do this, and, if he is, should be

115

depended on to a far greater degree than even the pediatrician for such advice, because medical doctors deal with the whole gamut of human ills, while the otologist deals with diseases of the ear, and only the audiologist is concerned with hearing loss as such and its impact on the individual.

But so long as communication remains an obstacle, one cannot expect to fully use the skills and experience that audiology has provided. In fact, the mere fact that the communication barrier exists serves to discredit the profession. How can one accept any advice from an expert who cannot communicate with the people he professes to be expert upon? Thus, it would seem that the first requirement would be to break down the communication barrier. Once this barrier is down, it is very possible that people who have not had any contact with the profession since they left school might be persuaded to make spasmodic, if not regular, visits to see if something has not been devised that might help them alleviate their handicap. However, the most important segments of the hearing-impaired population are the very young and, if not very old, people who have begun to experience deterioration of hearing later in life. Both these groups require more than the mere diagnosis of loss, or the type and degree of loss. They need expert guidance on how to cope with that loss and on what the effect such loss will have in many areas of their lives.

I am reminded of the last time I had an audiological examination. It was a routine one, for the verification of my deafness as part of the vocational rehabilitation procedure. At that time I had been deaf for more than twenty years. The audiologist's recommendations, which accompanied the audiogram, said, "Learn lipreading." While I did not make an issue of it, I wondered what he thought I was using to communicate with him at the time, and it seemed to me a mighty casual way to deal with what would have been a real shock to someone else.

As I said earlier, the audiologist is the most logical source of information regarding the effects of hearing loss to the largest segments of our hearing-impaired population and, as such, has a tremendous responsibility to know as much as possible about things that are of particular concern to both the parents of the very young and the older person whose life is changing or will be changed as the result of hearing loss.

The reference to lipreading is a case in point. Without going into the issue of methodology, the failure to inform parents of the different schools of thought regarding this controversy has and will continue to damage many young children and their parents. In some instances, for example, where parents are aware that their children are not progressing in a satisfactory manner, they are unable to do anything, because they know nothing of the alternatives that are available.

As one parent put it, I could see that my son was not making satisfactory progress, but I blamed it on the school and took him from school to school seeking satisfaction. I never realized that it was the method that was holding him back. I always thought it was the school." And the reason she failed to realize it was the method and not the school was she never knew there was another method.

In other instances, parents are specifically warned against the use of manual communication and told that use of sign language would inhibit, if not prevent entirely, the development of a child's speech and speech-reading capabilities. Yet we have considerable evidence to indicate that this is not so. In fact, it is our belief that, if a deaf child is permitted the use of sign language, or rather what we call Total Communication, and this is used by all members of the family all the time, not just when communicating with him, then the reverse might be true and his speech and speechreading abilities will be far superior to the pure oralist. First, because he will have more and better input, and second, because it would be relatively easy to communicate with all members of his family, a greater willingness to *attempt* to communicate. I do not believe it is necessary to touch on the *desire* to communicate. This is self-evident and what limits communication is the ability to do so, or the inability if you wish. Drs. Vernon, Mindel, Schlessinger, Stuckless and Birch, Quigley, and others, have demonstrated conclusively that sign language does not necessarily have any adverse effect on speech or speechreading. Further insofar as I am aware, there is no research that indicates that the use of manual communication *does* inhibit speech. This myth has developed from the fact that many deaf people do not speak, once they learn there are other ways to communicate. That much is true. What is overlooked, or perhaps ignored, is that anyone can find it easy to hate that which is forced upon them. You could learn to hate steak if you were forced into having it as a steady diet, so why should it be improbable that the deaf child comes early to hate speech? It is not that it is difficult, it is the steady diet he got when he was too little to rebel that does it.

Today, there has been some modification of the oral-only position, and parents are advised that if or when it becomes apparent that the child cannot succeed orally, then sign language is acceptable. What parent will accept manual communication under those conditions? Who wants to admit that their child cannot make the grade and must settle for less than the best? And what seems to be worse is that no one is advised of the consequences of failure. I wonder how many parents would be so anxious for speech and speechreading, if they knew that but one in four can make a go of it by this method, and that the three who do not succeed orally will be put at an educational disadvantage which will hamper them all the days of their lives.

In relation to the preceding statement, it is taken from the Life Science Library on Sound and Hearing, which acknowledges assistance from the leading oral schools for the deaf in this country. This volume does not state that failure will put the child at a serious disadvantage, but it does say that only one out of four deaf children can be taught to speak intelligibly. While it is entirely possible that the lure of speech and speechreading is so great that some, perhaps even many, parents will shoot for the moon and hang the consequences; still it is only fair that they be made aware of the consequences before having to make such a decision.

Parents need, at times, to be reminded also that childhood is but a small part of an individual's life span; that as a child, he can depend on his parents to supply any of the needs that he cannot provide for himself. As a child he can depend on his parents to take over in any extraordinary situation where speech and speechreading will not serve. For example, how well would you expect lipreading to serve when one is ill and in pain? If you are dealing with a child, you ask his parents. But when you are dealing with an adult, do you ask his children? Or worse yet, you are dealing with a child whose parents are deaf, who are distraught, worried, and scarcely able to concentrate on anything except the fact that their child is ill and in pain. What good is lipreading then? What good is lipreading when you have undergone surgery for cataracts and both your eyes are bandaged? Or when you are in the operating room where the surgeon is trying to tell you something with his mouth covered by a surgical mask?

These are but a few of the more dramatic incidents that occur in adulthood. There are many other problems which can and do have serious consequences. Instructions from a doctor, for instance. Lipreading is admittedly a hazardous game at best. Can one be sure of what the doctor said? Did he say 15 to 50? What is worse is that the widespread belief in the efficacy of lipreading encourages the doctor to deliver his instructions orally, completely and perhaps blissfully unaware that there is a very good chance his patient doesn't understand a word of what he is saying.

In summary, I would like to repeat that it seems to me that the audiologist is the logical person to be the authority on deafness. His concern is much more specific than that of a doctor, pediatrician, or even an otologist, and, therefore, the depth of his knowledge must be much greater than is presently the case. He needs to know not only all aspects of methodology, but also the kinds of problems and needs that beset the deaf child and the deaf adult. And more importantly, he must be ready to share his knowledge with parent or patient as the case may be, because both are equally bewildered by the magnitude of the problems with which they are faced and because of their bewilderment, frustration and concern may not have wit to ask or to be interested in anything but the immediate problem.

The mother of a young deaf child is trying to cope with a situation for which there is no preparation, for which no one but you can help at the time. Educators help, but that comes later, while the older person sees his world crumbling, perhaps his job is going, certainly his social life is suffering, and there is little or nothing he can find that will tell him how to cope. There is only you. Whether this is the most desirable situation is open to question. Still, someone must be knowledgeable about these problems. There must be someone to whom all these people, who may have only occasional contact with deafness, can turn. It is unreasonable to expect in depth knowledge from pediatricians, only a few of whom may even have deaf patients; or hospitals where one or two may be admitted annually for reasons unrelated to their hearing loss or even lawyers, other law enforcement personnel, whose contact will be minimal at best. But it is not unreasonable to suggest that there should be qualified, professionally trained people to whom other professions can turn when the need arises. It is also reasonable to say that, as professional people whose concern deals primarily with hearing and hearing loss, audiologists should provide the expertise.

I would add but one more thing and that is, if what I have said rings true, and if audiology accepts the challenge to provide this expertise, I hope no one will be tempted to use this expertise "to play God." By that I mean deciding what information should be given and what should be withheld. Advice, yes. We all need advice, but we also need some way of making our own decisions, of deciding for ourselves whether to accept or reject the advice that is given, and we can only do this by having it all, the pros and the cons.

Deaf Consumerism

Keynote address, February 1977.

A couple of years ago in preparing my first keynote address, they told me that the function of a keynoter was to generate enthusiasm, stimulate thinking, in short, set the participants on fire. I didn't do so well then. But tonight I am ready—see, I've brought my own matches! But seriously, I am pleased to be here. I am especially pleased to have this topic. Consumerism, particularly deaf consumerism, is a subject that is dear to me. It is also something that I had been advocating since I was old enough to know what the word was supposed to mean.

While it has been only recently that the government and other providers of service have come to acknowledge the value of consumer input, the idea has been with us for a long time. I guess there are many cliches that exemplify this. In particular the one that goes, "You can lead a horse to water, but you can't make him drink." That and the other old standby, "The customer is always right," are as explicit examples of consumerism as anyone could ask for. I would say that the former is the reason you are here now. It certainly was the motivating factor in developing deaf consumerism as we know it today. I do not recall just when this took place, but I remember that it was in the early sixties when the leaders in the deaf community and the providers of services became increasingly aware that the programs that were so painstakingly developed to meet the needs of deaf people were failing. Adult education programs were not taking hold, rehabilitation projects were not meeting their goals despite the fact they were carefully planned by people who were knowledgeable in their fields.

In fact, this was happening everywhere, not only in deafness but with all other disabilities. With it came the belated realization that, as with leading horses to water, it was and is possible to develop ideal programs, perfect programs, the kind of programs that exactly fill the needs of the deaf community or any other community—but if that consumer didn't want them, they wouldn't work. This is what I think created the interest in consumerism as it is practiced today.

Momentum for consumerism was provided by the Black Movement. The black people proved that a strong and united thrust could move mountains. They also provided some valuable lessons in showing that one could get the support of non-black people in their objectives and possibly have shown some of the negative aspects of such a movement, depending on how you look at it. One of those effects was the culmination where the black people said to their white supporters, "You helped us get to where we are today, to the point that we can think for ourselves, speak for ourselves, fight for ourselves, now get out of the way and let us do it." This, I am sure, came as a shock to many people, but it is a natural result of evolution. It comes as naturally as the day comes when the child says to its parents, "I am no longer a child, I am a person. As a person I will make my own life, my own decisions, I will fight my own battles, I need you but not for that."

The rise of deaf consumerism on the other hand was slower, more difficult to achieve. It is safe to say that even now when consumer activities are the rule rather than the exception, there are many deaf people who worry about what consumerism is and where it will lead to. For too many years, the deaf child and the deaf adult have been led to believe that they should be grateful for small blessings and should keep a low profile. They were not advised to do so on the basis of the "meek shall inherit the earth." It was more implicit that they were educated, employed, and in fact permitted to exist on sufferance. That the greater world of the hearing has given and having given, could and would, if sufficiently provoked, take away those crumbs that deaf people were being permitted to take from the hearing table.

I can remember very well, the astonishment and shock that greeted my first suggestion to the Office of Vocational Rehabilitation for consumer input. When I suggested that the NAD should be permitted to review proposals in the area of deafness with a view to advising on their relevancy, "Do you mean the NAD should decide which proposals our agency should fund?" I was asked. And I said, "No, but our input should help the agency make this determination." If our input was wrong, we would learn. If our input was right but disregarded, VRA would learn, and if the agency didn't learn soon enough, it probably could use new personnel. While I called that consumerism, other people called it militancy. But no matter what label you put on it, it was a radical departure from tradition which said deaf people should be seen but not heard (no pun intended).

This attitude created and still creates problems. Prior to the 1960's, the general feeling among the deaf leadership was "independence or bust." In particular, the thinking then was that not only should they not demand anything from the government, but they should not even accept anything. Possibly this stems from the fact that many of the deaf leaders were union printers, and unions are very suspicious of federal intervention in their internal affairs. Possibly, too, that was compounded by the educational philosophy that said, whatever the deaf people want done, they should do it. This line led, I am sure, to the rejection of any additional tax exemption such as accrues to the blind and to the notion that government aid would make deaf people second-class citizens.

Probably the most controversial of all discussions came from Stahl Butler who dared to take the word "charity" and say that much of what we used to call "charity" isn't. That deaf people have the same right to the services that are available, as non-deaf people have. And that community funding to meet the needs of its citizens was not charity in the sense of a few rich people tossing pennies to a crowd of starving beggars. A program of using community resources to meet the needs of its people—whether these are needs of some of the people or all of the people–was not charity but common sense. Such heretical thinking created an uproar. Deaf people throughout the nation praised or reviled him; there was no middle ground. In one sense this rationale led to what I still think was the turning point for consumerism. That was the workshop on Community Development Through Organizations of and for the Deaf. It was coordinated by Alan B. Crammatte, of Gallaudet College. This historic meeting was held at Old Point Comfort, in Virginia, and is most commonly referred to as the Fort Monroe Workshop. The workshop is the source for such ideas as the Leadership Training Program, at CSUN, and the new Leadership Deaf program sponsored jointly by Gallaudet College and the NAD. It also conceptualized the Council of Organizations Serving the Deaf.

More than that, however, it sparked the peaceful revolution which led to the first change in NAD administration in 18 years. By 1964, the NAD had a new administration and a new policy that fairly reeked of militancy as compared to traditional practices.

This did not come easy. Many deaf people were hesitant and doubting. Among the admonitions and fears of the membership were: "Remember, the NAD is an organization for adults. Leave education alone, concentrate on the needs of the adult population. That is where the NAD belongs." But as most people know, the adult, by and large, is what education makes him or her. If we are to meet the needs of the deaf adult, we have to be involved in every stage of his/her development—sort of a womb-to-the-tomb approach. That evokes laughs, but it is no laughing matter. As consumers today, we are pressing hard, for example, for an Institute for the Prevention of Deafness, which could roughly correspond to the womb, and we also advocate expanded programs for the aging, which I suppose is about as close to the tomb as one would care to get.

Another general comment as I have already noted was: "Don't accept governmental assistance. If you accept government aid, then deaf people will become second-class citizens and in time the government will take over your organization." Again our policy disagreed. It was and is our contention—in fact our entire democracy is based on the concept—that the government is the servant of the people, and you measure your status by the amount of service you get.

When it comes down to it, we got a lot. Stahl Butler in his paper at Fort Monroe, "Putting First Things First," said, "As I have written before, Vocational Rehabilitation is the third best friend of the deaf, third only to schools and the sign language." Today many people put Vocational Rehabilitation first. Possibly this is because we take Sign Language for granted now. But moving Vocational Rehabilitation ahead of schools is the result of consumerism. Deaf consumers have a vastly greater input into the rehabilitation process than any other agency of government on any level. This is not intended to say that we are satisfied with rehabilitation agencies or that we feel that we are getting either the quality or quantity of services to which we are entitled. But we are heard and appreciate it! This is what consumerism is all about. We do attempt to get more input into the Office of Education. We have made a little progress there. For the past decade, deaf evaluators have had a major role in selecting the feature films that are captioned by Media Services and Captioned Films. We have pride in the fact that Dr. Malcolm Norwood, who is deaf, is head of that division and that the Office of Education has the only Civil Service rated interpreter for the deaf in the country on its staff. But I believe we feel we should have a much greater involvement in the educational process than we have now.

In spite of all the progress we are making, we have many hangups that need to be cured. One of them, and a major one, is the carryover from our "don't-rock-the-boat" days. This is best evidenced by our reactions to the Black Power movement. We have learned a great deal from what the black people have accomplished, but we shy away from calling a spade a spade. We say "Deaf Pride" when we mean "Deaf Power," and we claim that we only want qualified deaf people to be appointed to positions of authority, when we know that we ought to be out there asking, "How many deaf people are on your staff? How many are in supervisory capacity? Never mind the qualifications, hire the right number or there will be trouble." Mind you, I am not saying that what we are now doing is wrong, but it is not the way we feel in our hearts we should go.

Even those of us who think we are pretty sophisticated in the area of consumerism have to pause every now and then to assess where we are and how much of our thinking is influenced by our education and training and how much by what we consider are the mistakes of the people we are trying to emulate.

Generally, accepted leaders in the deaf community have tried to choose a middle path. They are not so militant as to want to picket everybody at the drop of a hat. Certainly no one at all has ever even thought of violence. They are not as meek as before, either, sitting around in circles bemoaning to each other that the deaf community is always being ignored.

Today we are speaking out. We are trying to make our views known and heeded. We are more aggressive in not waiting to be asked or invited to give our views. We are demanding that those views be heard and considered. We are also beginning to take our grievances to the courts. We have always felt that, in the long run, the only way to effect major changes would be through the courts, and, as the saying goes, "The longest journey in life begins with the first step." We have taken that step.

Deafness, like many other minority issues, has a history of extremes. We are engaged in many controversies—oralism, manualism, Uncle Tomism, independence, dependence; you name it, we have it! It is a proven law of nature that a pendulum must swing from one extreme to the other, if it is really a pendulum worth its salt. Today our pendulum has swung. We are becoming much more militant—at times when militancy is called for. We have swung from the position of going it alone, every man for himself, to togetherness. We have coalitions and councils, and we are perhaps back where we were in the days of the American Revolution, when Ben Franklin said it best, "We must all hang together lest we all hang separately." We have taken that first step there, too, with the creation of American Coalition of Citizens with Disabilities. The deaf consumer is learning that with his two good legs he can help push the wheelchair of the person whose two good ears can serve as his or whose voice can be his voice when a loud voice is needed. One thing is certain, the deaf person has learned he is a person with all the rights, privileges, and responsibilities of a member of the human race, and he will not ever again let anyone forget it.

To Russia—With Love

Reprinted from Deaf American, *November 1978.*

Readers of James Bond stories may recognize the title, and I am a little concerned that I may be getting into trouble for plagiarism. However, in this case, the title is intended to be taken literally. The writer, as reported elsewhere, has just returned from a visit to Russia where he had gone in company with three of the most prominent leaders of the deaf community—Boyce R. Williams, the director of the Deafness and Communications Disorders Office of the Rehabilitation Services Administration, Department of Health, Education and Welfare, a title which, by itself, ought to impress people who are not familiar with the accomplishments of our special leader in the field of deafness rehabilitation; Dr. Edward C. Merrill, Jr., the president of Gallaudet College and the recipient of the 1978 NAD Distinguished Service Award, which is the highest honor we have to bestow on anyone; and Dr. William Castle, the director of the National Technical Institute for the Deaf, and one of our principal benefactors at the same convention this summer, where he placed the resources of the NTID at our disposal, insuring that we had one of the most successful conventions in our history. So, it is obvious that I have not understated in saying that I was in the company of three of the most prominent leaders in the country in the area of deafness.

We journeyed to Russia at the invitation of Vladimir Fufaev, the president of the All Russia Society for the Deaf. Fufaev was also a member of the Bureau of the World Federation of the Deaf, and, during time the author also served on the Bureau, had worked closely together, disregarding the politics that have plagued both countries, because in deafness, there are no politics. We are interested only in easing the plight of deaf people the world over. Actually, this visit was long in materializing. From 1971 through 1975, whenever Fufaev and I met, he was continually urging that we visit Russia, to study what is being done in that country, and perhaps benefit from some of the things that he felt were being handled better there than here. He also acknowledged that he felt that some of the things we do here are better than that done in his country, so that mutual assistance would benefit both countries, and other countries as well, because the demonstration of cooperative efforts between organizations of deaf people from countries of so different political philosophies could not but impress the other nations to the thought that our interest in seeking to upgrade deafness and deaf people transcended the political implications of our respective governments.

Most of the time, we were unable to respond since such a project (visiting Russia and the obligations that we would incur in so doing) would require a large sum of money that we did not have and probably would

125

not have in the foreseeable future. But by 1976, it appeared that such a visit might be financed, and we sought and received a formal invitation to make such a visit. Unfortunately, between the time that the request for a formal invitation was made, and the time we actually received this invitation, our funding sources dried up and we were left with an invitation to which we could not respond. Intermittently, from 1976 to 1978, we received letters and cablegrams asking when we were coming, showing that the Russian association was sincerely interested in having us visit their country and looking forward to the visit. Finally, with the aid and support of Gallaudet College and the National Technical Institute for the Deaf, a means was developed whereby we were able to deal with future financial commitments, and we were able to respond affirmatively. We were coming with only the determination of when to come being up in the air.

Considering that we, Boyce Williams, Edward Merrill, Bill Castle and myself, were a diverse group with diverse interests, it was somewhat difficult to focus on a time frame that would satisfy everybody. Drs. Merrill and Castle, as one might expect, were interested in going at a time when they could observe the school system in action. Dr. William's interest lay more in the employment and rehabilitation programs, while I was especially interested in the activities of the Society itself, and how we might use some of their programs for the benefit of the deaf people of America. But, with a great deal of compromising on everyone's part, a target date of September 11-22, 1978, was set and we communicated this to Mr. Fufaev, noting that we would like specifically to visit schools for the deaf, their rehabilitation center, their factories and clubs for the deaf, as well as the Society for the Deaf itself, although we were already in the habit of calling it the "Association of the Deaf" despite the fact that the official title was the All Russia Society for the Deaf.

The letter of intent was mailed in July, along with a request for assistance in expediting the acquisition of visas and any other aid we might need to secure permission to go into the country. Like most Americans, the stories of Russian rigidity was well-known to us, and we anticipated problems in getting permission to enter the country. As time went by with no response, we became concerned that the mission might have to be cancelled because we could not get visas in time. Finally, roughly 21 days before our scheduled departure, a cablegram arrived responding positively to our letter and the wheels were in motion. First, there were the requirements for applying for a visa. These included three photographs, a letter from a travel agency regarding our itinerary, all of which had to be presented at least 14 days prior to departure. So, we, all of us, rushed to the Russian Consulate in order to get under the wire. But things were not to be that simple.

First, my administrative assistant, Liz DeMarco, had car trouble and was stranded in her apartment. Since she had all of the information on the trip, I rushed to pick her up and in my haste, what was supposed to be a 20-minute trip, took an hour and a half. This resulted in calling Gallaudet to ask that Dr. Merrill's papers be delivered directly to the consulate as we would not have time to pick them up. Then Dr. Castle's papers, which were to have been delivered by air express, did not arrive, and finally, returning to my car to head for the consulate with minutes to spare, the car wouldn't start. Frantically borrowing another car, we dashed off with little hope that we could make the consulate in time to beat its one o'clock closing. To top it all off, we missed the street on which the consulate is located, and, after searching futilely for it and stopping twice to ask for directions, we finally arrived—at 1:03 p.m. and, to be sure, the consulate was closed.

Having heard all kinds of things about Russian rigidity, we were prepared for anything, and on the following morning were discussing strategy in the event that the Russians were to be unyielding about the 14-day requirement. Dr. Williams, his secretary, Charlotte Coffield, Mrs. Williams, Liz and I, all turned up at the consulate at 9:30 a.m. About an hour later a special messenger from NTID arrived with Dr. Castle's papers and, believe it or not, all was roses. The consulate had a file on the trip that was thicker than my own. All smiles and collaboration, they advised that the visas would be ready on September 5, which was Labor Day and all we had to do was to come and pick them up. So, finally, we were off. We had time to make some preparations for the trip. Noting that the temperature in Russia at this time of the year was somewhat colder than in Washington, we checked into our wardrobes, and failing to find suitable topcoats, settled for a raincoat and a sweater, which was fortunate, because it rains a lot in Russia at this time of the year.

Finally, the great day approached. We gathered at Dulles Airport ready to board our flight, which we thought at least was to take us direct to Frankfurt, Germany, and thence to Moscow. The first disillusionment came when the flight was delayed. For some reason it has been my experience that no transatlantic flight ever leaves on time, and this one was no exception. Finally, after about an hour's delay, we boarded the plane and flew to New York where we changed planes and boarded a Pan American 747 for the trip to Frankfurt. This plane was also delayed with the result that we did not arrive in Frankfurt early enough to take advantage of its duty-free shop, but instead, were quickly herded aboard another much smaller plane for the trip to Moscow, finally arriving in that city at 4 p.m. on September 12, almost a full day after we left Washington. Of course, this was misleading because of the time change, but it was something that we had not calculcated on in reporting our plans to the All Russia Society for the Deaf.

Emerging from the gates in Moscow's airport, I saw Fufaev anxiously scanning faces and breaking into a smile as he recognized me. As we lined up at passport control, he told me in sign language that he had expected us the day before and was worried about what had happened to us since we had not shown, until he realized we had probably forgotten that in traveling East, we would add many hours to the trip. With Fufaev's help we moved rapidly through the formalities, passport control, customs, money declaration and the like. Being engrossed in talking with Fufaev, whom I have known for more than five years, I paid little attention to any of the proceedings to my later regret. But at the time, he was accompanied by two other people, Edward Vartanian, a hearing man who is Vice Editor-in-Chief of V EDINOM STROYER, which translated out roughly into A UNITED FRONT, and is the All Russia's version of THE DEAF AMERICAN magazine. Also a young lady by the name of Galina who was an employee of Intourist, the Russian travel agency that regulates all travel by foreigners in that country. We never did get her last name, but Galina was to accompany us throughout our stay in Russia.

Finally we were out. Galina had a bunch of carnations in her hand, and at Fufaev's directions, gave them all to me while Fufaev asked that I share them with my companions. So I split the bunch and each of us had a couple while we left the airport and were ushered into cabs that were to take us to a hotel in Moscow to rest and have dinner in preparation for departing that night for Leningrad. At the hotel, Fufaev asked for my passport and that of Boyce since they had reserved two rooms for us in which to relax until dinner time around nine p.m. So I surrendered my passport.

A few minutes later there was a request for my visa which I did not have. Since the visa was on a separate piece of paper, not stamped in my passport as had been done in the past, I did not notice it being returned to me nor did I expect to get it back. So we made frantic calls to the airport and luckily enough it had been found and was in passport control. I had to go back to the airport to pick it up. In this effort I was accompanied by an interpreter from the All Russia Society whose name is Tanya. Tanya has deaf parents and is not only a good sign language interpreter but is also fluent in English, more fluent I think than Galina, for she was the only person in Russia that spoke English who I could lipread. We drove to the airport in Fufaev's car and retrieved the visa and then returned to the hotel just about time for dinner.

Dinner was a gay affair. The hotel dining room was crowded with people. There was a band and a lot of dancing. We had a truly elaborate meal, one of the many that were to come. Featured at the meal, incidentally, were some things that we came to conclude were staples in the Russian diet. First of course, was the vodka. Russian people love vodka and to be honest, so do we. Also there was cole slaw, cucumbers in sour cream and caviar. Caviar in Russia is both red and black. Frankly, I hate caviar or anything that comes out of the sea. But in trying not to be an "Ugly American" I manfully forced some of the red caviar down my throat and it did not actually kill me. The food was good and we enjoyed watching the dancers. A nearby table yielded a friend of Fufaev's whose name I did not catch when he was introduced. A short time later, another bottle of vodka arrived at the table and then it was time for us to leave for the railroad station and our trip to Leningrad.

The railroad station was bustling with activities although it was almost midnight. Again we went in three cars—two cabs and Vladimir Fufaev's car which, by the way, was chauffer driven. On the way I was told that there were several railroad stations in Moscow and this one was the one that handled trains between Leningrad and Moscow (and probably other points along that general line but my geography is lousy). As noted, Galina and Edward were to accompany us. Pete Merrill and I shared a compartment and Boyce and Bill Castle shared another. At the stroke of midnight the train took off. Possibly due to the need to run back and forth after my visa, I was tired enough to sleep well. None of the others did, however, so that it was a pretty tired bunch of Americans that arrived in Leningrad that morning.

In Leningrad we were met by the president of the Leningrad Society for the Deaf, Aleksander Lopatin who sported steel caps on his teeth and had a remarkable resemblance to Mervin Garretson, the Immediate Past President of the National Association of the Deaf. Lopatin and his assistants escorted us to our hotel which was to be our home for the next seven days. The name of the hotel translated out into something like the Soryata or some such, and during the exploration of Leningrad and environs, it often occurred to me that if I were to get lost I would never find my way around the city or even back to the hotel.

Fortunately this did not happen, so I am back safe and sound. Lopatin was a very good host and I found it easy to communicate with him in a combination of Gestuno, Russian, English and American sign language. In both Leningrad and Moscow, our hosts had laid out an agenda based largely on what I had written to Fufaev back in July. All of these items were on the agenda. In addition, our hosts had arranged for us to do the usual tourist bit, but in our case, by private taxi rather than the inevitable tourist buses that one can find everywhere in Europe on both sides of the Iron Curtain.

One of the places we visited was the Leningrad version of Arlington Cemetery. This is an especially revered place for the people of Russia, for here are buried thousands of people who died during World War II in the siege of Leningrad by Hitler's Germany. In the picture you can see from left to right, Pete Merrill explaining to me what it is all about with Galina in the middle, while Edward and Aleksander, at the extreme right, watch. Since Bill Castle took the picture, that left Boyce wandering someplace nearby. Much of the sightseeing focused on historical places with a great emphasis on the damage that was done by the Germans in World War II. Many of the places and churches showed intensive damage, and where the restoration had been completed, there were photographs showing what the rooms looked like before the damage was repaired. We

129

visited many famous places; the Fortress of Peter and Paul in Leningrad; the old city of Novgorod where some of the more interesting history of Russia took place and which is pictured here.

This picture is of the honor guard, somewhat similar to the Honor Guard at the Tomb of the Unknown Soldier in Arlington Cemetery. But in this case, the guards are high school students of Novgorod. According to the interpreter, each high school stands guard for one week of the year. Note that the front two students are boys and armed. The one in the rear is a girl and ostensibly she is in command of the trip. The guards change every 15 minutes in an elaborate ceremony. When we passed by, the guards demanded that our cab drivers remove their hats which they did promptly. Fortunately, none of the Americans except Boyce had a hat to remove so we did not violate protocol. This picture shows the Novgorod Kremlin. Apparently Kremlin means "Capitol" or something because there are several Kremlins and the one that we hear about here in America is in Moscow. But this is where the eternal flame and the guards are stationed. There are several eternal flames like this in various parts of Russia, one in the cemetery previously mentioned.

Then we visited our first objective, a preschool program for hard of hearing children. This was housed in a large building that was converted into a school. The children were taught by a combination of speech, auditory training and fingerspelling. It was one thing that we found in Russia that seemed to make more sense than what we do here in America. In Russia the hearing impaired are all given special education with the determination of who is hearing impaired and who is deaf being decided by a combination of factors including, and emphasizing, the ability to speak. As near as I was able to understand, the Russians consider the ability to speak very important. They do not, as is done in the United States, stress speech as necessary to be integrated into a hearing world. In fact it did not seem to me that they cared a hoot about the hearing world. However, like in many other areas, the philosophy seemed to go back to a time long removed from the 20th century. As expounded by Aristotle, they feel that the key to intelligence lies in speech, or in other words, the mouth is the gateway to the brain. I have some private determination that when the Russians come to visit us in 1980, I will make a special effort to expose them to the many highly educated and highly competent nonspeaking deaf people we have in this country.

Still, it was a revelation. The young kids did very well in class although we did not really have a basis for comparison, as the children we saw were not deaf, but had varying degrees of hearing loss. Still they were comfortable in their environment and obviously at ease. Our next visit was to the club or cultural center in Leningrad. This was located in a large mansion which was the former home of a cousin of Czar Nicholas II. The place is very elaborate. It contained a ballroom, an auditorium, television room and lecture hall, a small library, as well as other rooms that we did not actually get to see. According to Aleksander, the club in Leningrad has 7,000 members who pay a nominal sum, roughly 50 cents a year, in dues.

The clubs do not sell alcoholic beverages although such things as snacks, tea and coffee are available. Aleksander also said that attendance at club functions was great, so great that the present club was inadequate and his society was in the process of building a larger one which would be ready for occupancy in 1980. But the club had a full-time staff which seemed to vary. In Leningrad the director of the club was deaf and her assistant hearing. In Moscow it was the other way around with the director hearing and his assistant a deaf woman. But in all cases, everyone was fluent in sign language, despite the edict that the use of manual communication is not needed in Russia and does not take place after the deaf child reaches fourth grade.

In Leningrad we also visited one of the 70 "enterprises" that are under the All Russia Society. This was a factory that made amplifiers for motion picture projectors. According to Aleksander, the factory has 900 employees, of whom 750 are deaf. He told me that the deaf and hearing workers were paid the same but that the deaf workers had a production quota that was 10% less than the hearing. The director of the factory was hearing, but it was my understanding that Aleksander was his boss. The workers appeared quite happy and satisfied. I was able to talk with some of them and they told me that some of the hearing people could sign, but not all. They also were fascinated by the Americans and particularly by Pete Merrill's Polaroid camera which he let me borrow to take pictures of some of the workers in the factory.

As is usual in the deaf community, word of the camera spread like wildfire and everywhere we went we were asked to take pictures. I talked with a number of the workers. One woman told me she had worked in the factory for 20 years and was quite content with what she was doing. All of the people seemed to be that way. We noted that there were training components in the plants so that workers could be trained and upgraded.

Between times we were still going sightseeing. One of the most interesting places was the palace of Peter the Great. Peter appears to be one of the most progressive of the Russian czars and his palace reflects a great deal of what the man was like. This picture shows the palace and a few of the fountains which abound on the grounds. The other picture shows all of us, Edward, Aleksander, Fred, Pete and Galina, in front of another of the fountains on the grounds of the palace. Hidden behind Galina is the local guide. I forget how many fountains there are on the grounds, but there are more than one hundred of them including some sneaky ones.

Apparently Peter the Great was also a practical joker because in some places there are piles of rocks which, when stepped on, activate hidden

131

fountains. In another part of the grounds there is a sort of summer hut or gazebo which, when enough people gather in, it activates another fountain that stays on until enough people get out to lighten it enough, so somebody has to get wet. We saw them in operation. Another fountain which was not operating was activated by a bench in a secluded nook and I cannot imagine how many prospective couples found their ardor cooled by an unexpected shower when they sat on the bench.

Another trip from Leningrad was to Pavlovsk. This is a suburb of Leningrad and the home of the Rehabilitation Institute that we wanted to see. The director of the Rehabilitation Center is Josef Gjelman who is also a member of the World Federation of the Deaf's Sign Language Commission and probably the leading authority on sign language in Russia. Dr. Gjelman is also one of the most fluent users of Gestuno in the world, and for me at least the easiest to understand. At his institute we were exposed to many fascinating examples of what they do in Russia. The pictures here are those of student artists at the center. Probably due to the nature of the general Russian society, art is a good field and many of the students display great talent in this field. The other picture is of the class in interpreting. Russia, like the United States, provides special training for interpreters for the deaf and here are some of them with Professor Gjelman shown in the background in the center and Boyce Williams on the right.

Looking at the girls, one is struck by the different characteristics shown. Blondes, redheads, brunettes and all reflecting the wide range of ethnic races to be found in the USSR. Also shown here is Bill Castle, Galina and Pete Merrill in Dr. Gjelman's office where he was explaining the activities of the Rehabilitation Center and making us welcome. As with the other places we visited, each of us received gifts from our hosts and at this center, in particular, some of the gifts we received were things made by the center's students.

One of the main interests which we were unable to satisfy was the desire for sign language books. Dr. Merrill was fortunate in having brought to Russia a supply of Lottie Riekehof's book, "The Joy of Signing," which Dr. Gjelman was delighted to receive. We were only able to spend two hours in the center which caused our host to remark that things were at least improving because in 1975, while attending the World Congress in Washington, he could only spend an hour and a half at Gallaudet, but here we made it two hours. So we left, promising that when he came to the United States again in 1980, he would have at least a whole day at Gallaudet.

Finally, on Sunday, prior to departing for Moscow, we returned again to visit the Leningrad Club for the Deaf. Only a couple hundred people were there due to some miscalculation on the part of Aleksander who suggested we forego visiting the club on Saturday night because that was the night captioned films were shown and many of the members would

132

stay home and watch television. So instead of going to the club on Saturday, we went to the Leningrad ballet and watched some of the old dances which went over very well with both Boyce and I, although we aren't exactly musical. But at the club on Sunday, we were able to look briefly into an interpreted film in the small theater. This film was not captioned, but instead, one of the student interpreters from the Rehabilitation Center in Pavlovsk sat nearby under a bright light and interpreted the dialogue.

Then there was to be a dance, but in the meanwhile, Pete Merrill, Boyce and I, with the help of Aleksander, were talking with the club members, both asking and answering questions about life in Russia and the United States. Bill Castle, who does very well by the Russian language, had a ball by himself talking with the members in Russian. Finally, it all ended and we were whisked back to our hotel for a final banquet farewell ceremony prior to a return to the railroad and the trip back to Moscow. It was a gala affair. We felt that we had established some good relations and could look forward to the day that our Leningrad hosts would be visiting with us in America. Again, at midnight, our train pulled out for Moscow which was eight hours away.

(The article notes at its end, "To be continued." But it was not.)

You Don't Have to Be Old to Be Smart!

Fred wrote this guest editorial for the Junior Deaf American. *It appeared in January, 1979.*

A good many years ago, as a young man, I was convinced that there was no substitute for experience. It was my feeling at the time that because I was young and because I was just out of school, there were many things that I did not know; many things that people who had been around longer than I knew more about and to whom I should listen and follow because of their experience and knowledge, which far outweighed anything that I had. This feeling, I find, is not unusual. There are many young people today who have the same feeling of inadequacy in the face of older people who keep saying things like "you are too young," or "you have no experience," or "you don't know what you are talking about." While it was proven that this is sometimes the case, it does not follow automatically that you have to be old to be smart. It does not follow that experience is the beginning and end to all human endeavor and, as young people, it seems to me that you need to keep a number of things very firmly in mind.

The first of these is that age has no corner on brains. On the other hand it is true, and one has to keep in mind that we learn from our mistakes, so that the experience of the past can be and is a helpful guide to the future in the sense that people say, "Your idea is not workable. We tried that ten or fifteen years ago and it did not work. Since it did not work then, it will not work now." That may be true and it may not be true. When the NAD was established in 1880, no one dreamed that man would be able to fly or reach the moon or that you could go around the world in less than 24 hours. In 1880 that was impossible. Today it is common. In fact, it is safe to say that the day before the Wright Brothers took to the air at Kitty Hawk, North Carolina, it was impossible for man to fly. But 24 hours later the whole ball game changed and what was impossible yesterday not only became possible, but was a fact. We need to face the realization that, strictly speaking, nothing is impossible. It is not so much that things can or cannot be done as it is trying to find out just how they can be done. In working with people it has been my practice to say: "Don't tell me that it can't be done." I do not believe that there is anything that can't be done. What we need to do is to accept, first of all, that it can be done. That is half the battle already. Instead of wasting time discussing whether or not the idea is feasible, we start with knowing it can be done and spend our time trying to figure out how to do it. Of course, it does not always turn out that we are able to find the answer. Sometimes we find that no matter how hard we try, we do not come up with a way to meet our objective. Does that mean we have failed? Does it mean that the argument that nothing is impossible is wrong? I don't think so. I think that when we do not find out how to accomplish our goals, it means that we may be ahead of our time, or that science has not advanced far enough to do so the things that need to be done. But it does not mean that it is impossible—only that it may take longer than we think to do the job. There is a quotation that I like very much although I cannot remember where it came from. It goes like this: "The difficult we do now; the impossible takes a little longer."

That is the message I want to convey. Whatever happens will happen only if we act, and act intelligently. Nothing can't be done because you are young. Nothing will be done because one is old or young. The only way to get things done is to see what needs to be done. If it was tried before, see what may have been the reason for failure and try a new approach. But it is still true that it is better to try and fail than never to try at all.

Chapter IV
The Memorial Service

*O*n *Sunday, September 9, 1979, about four hundred of Fred's friends came together in the auditorium of the Model Secondary School for the Deaf, on the Gallaudet College campus. Fred requested that he have no funeral. His friends did not disappoint him. The service that day was not somber. Of course, tears spilled. But what took place was a celebration of life—Fred's life.*

The stage contained only a lectern at one end and a table at the other. On the table lay a dozen red roses next to a cut-crystal vase. As the speakers concluded their eulogies, they placed a rose in the vase.

The transcript of what they said is reproduced in the next pages. The reader must guess about the emotions of those who listened. Grief, true grief, is a private matter. Even when shared with hundreds, the feeling of loss has an inexpressible personal quality. On that day, in that packed auditorium, a common current flowed across the crowd. It accompanied the words that were spoken. But the words could not say enough. Still, they must do what they can to add a critical element to Fred's story—he was close to many people. While he lived, he was not a legend, a distant character, a symbol. He was, for many, a dear friend. And for a few, more than that.

Good afternoon, Friends of Fred.

It is a beautiful day to be remembering a splendid man. If you have come here to mourn Fred, please set aside such thoughts. For that was not Fred's nature. Humor was a very important part of his personality. Let us honor it by sharing memories of him.

Some twenty-five years ago, when Fred first came to Washington, he left his family in New York until he could make suitable arrangements. He shared an apartment with two young bachelors, one of whom was myself. As bachelors will do, we divided up the work. I couldn't cook so the other two did that and I cleaned up afterwards. I used to dread the days when it was Fred's turn. Not that he was a bad cook. It was just that he had the knack of using just about every pot, pan, and bowl in the kitchen. It mattered not what he cooked—be it steak or spaghetti—it seemed as if every single utensil was piled in the sink. That is my first memory of Fred.

Several months later, after his family was settled in Washington and I was living alone, he took me in. Perhaps he wanted to save me from slow starvation or perhaps he needed a now-expert dishwasher. I said he took me in. Those words do not describe it fully. For twelve years I was *a part* of the family—a time which I cherish and hold very dear.

You know that Kit and Fred have four children. This afternoon I would like to introduce myself to you as Jerry Jordan, the fifth child. Fred often referred to me in that way. And, indeed, he was a father to me. But, more than that, he was also the brother which I never had.

As our symbol this afternoon, we have chosen roses. Fred loved roses. He grew them in his yard and often brought them to the office. Perhaps I should be more accurate and say that he planted them and picked them but it was Kit who did the cultivating and weeding. Anyway, this beautiful vase, which belongs to his mother, represents the place in our heart where we want to preserve our memories of this dear friend. It is empty now. Each one of us wants to help fill this vase by sharing with you memories of the many facets of Fred.

For myself, this rose represents Fred, the father . . . and the brother.

—*Jerald M. Jordan*

Let us begin with a moment of silent prayer for the happy repose of the soul of Fred Schreiber. Please stand and bow your heads in silent prayer.

This is an honor to be able to pray and speak on your behalf for our friend Fred. All people who have come into contact with Fred, if only once, were in some way affected. They experienced his life filled with goodness, kindness, understanding, and love for his fellow man.

The virtue which we all loved in Fred was his ability to make everyone feel that he or she was his very personal friend. His attitude was the same towards all; he associated with the highest and the lowest in the same dignified manner. I recall the time he came to Louisiana to join parents of deaf children and deaf people themselves in their fight for better education. Without hesitating he grabbed a picket sign and joined the line shouting the loudest for improved education for the deaf. This is what made Fred a great leader. It is a lesson we can all learn that, as Fred, we must get down and do the work, never ashamed to get our hands dirty. During the last four NAD conventions I joined him almost every night until 1:00 or 2:00 in the morning printing the minutes and reports. This was the deaf leader working.

We often discussed religion when together: the similarities between his and mine, the religious needs of the deaf, the lack of religious service to the deaf individual and community. He had strong religious feelings and pride in his own Jewish faith.

Fred was a restless man. As Psalm 42 says, "His soul was thirsting for the Lord." He wanted to bring the beautiful of God's creation to all people. He expressed himself in a life dedicated to equality for his fellow man, whether it was in Louisiana fighting for equal education or removing barriers on the national level. Fred's dream was fulfilled in the signing of 504. And today 504 has reached paradise.

Fred's philosophy can best be summarized: "If one member is suffering due to inequities or injustices then we are all suffering, and we must work together to correct that."

His generosity knew no limits, giving of his time, money, and himself to others. I recall while interpreting for him in Rome he gave me his invitation to a private audience with the Pope. Even though he would have enjoyed it as much as I, he gave it up.

You all know how committed Fred was. I recall during a Communicative Skills Program Advisory Board meeting, in California in 1973, he was having his first heart attack, but he refused to do anything until the meeting was over. His service to man came before his own health. It can truly be said that Fred laid down his life for his friends.

Today we all join in prayer for Fred. May God welcome you into the company of Saints in the Kingdom of Light and Peace. And may the Angels lead you and take you to the Holy City, the New and Eternal Jerusalem. Amen.

—Reverend Gerard Howell

I stand here representing one of the most powerful consumer organizations in the world, the National Association of the Deaf. It has been around some 99 years but it was only during the last 20-25 years that it has become a very powerful voice for deaf people not only in this country but also in countries in other parts of the world. I can remember a time when there were very few agencies serving the deaf people: when a deaf person almost felt guilty for being a deaf person, when the language of sign was considered inferior, when there was no captioned news. When you could count rehabilitation counselors for the deaf on one hand and still have a few fingers to spare. And when deaf people were not consulted in the design of programs that were made for them. When Congress did not even know that they existed. When there were few books on deafness. And when the deaf community was not as well organized as it is now. Then things began to happen. Those things did not happen by themselves. It took many deaf individuals who cared enough to change things. One person stands far above all of us. That was Fred.

In the 1960's there was a man with vision who helped to bring the NAD to its present prominence (as it is today). In a short span of 20 years NAD grew from a kitchen-drawer operation to a large organization with a solid economic base. It required genius to accomplish this. Fred had it. Always he had to deal with 13 hard-headed, hard-nosed Board members, with delegates at every convention: Congress people, professional people, and the average deaf gal or guy on the street. He welded all these various elements into the very powerful organization that we know as NAD today. Fred was a product of the 1960's. Those years produced men like John F. Kennedy, Martin Luther King, and Whitney Young. There was so much going on at that time. Fred belonged to this same class of people who did something significant in life and made a lasting impact on the lives of people in a positive way. He became a symbol and model that helped the deaf men and women stand tall and walk proud. He knew how to communicate softly when possible and be tough if necessary. His presence commanded respect which caused people to listen and respect other deaf people. Many things about Fred are larger than life, but he was a real human being. He was warm, trusting; he laughed, he cried, he enjoyed, he became angry. He loved people and hoped people would love and respect him as he was. He could be tough if the situation demanded it. But deep down he was a soft touch. I personally knew many people whom he helped when they were down on their luck.

It is very difficult to say when Fred was happiest: in his boat on the bay, on the stage speaking to an audience, in a nightclub watching a show, or sitting alone wondering whether progress was being made in the lives of deaf people. Whatever it was that made him happiest, there is no question that he managed to live life to its fullest in every thing that he did. He had that one precious gift—a terrific sense of humor. As an administrator he was very fond of saying, "People should do things my way or the wrong way." I remember very clearly a time that I was asked on a very short notice to be M.C. for a banquet. I didn't have any new jokes, so I turned to Fred in desperation. He gave me right off the bat six or seven wonderful stories. Without question I was a wonderful M.C. That night everyone laughed at my jokes. I turned around and saw Fred. He was laughing so hard at all these stories, as if he were hearing them for the first time. I could not figure it out. Either he had a short memory or a big heart.

You could find him singing at the drop of a hat, any old time and place. You would find him singing "My Darling Clementine" so many times I am almost convinced that he wrote the words and composed the music for that song. What Fred said was almost always profound, but how he said it was not always profound. On a visit to CSUN his sign language skills were evaluated as being just a little bit above Bill Stevens' skills. When he got that rating he quickly wired Bill Stevens, congratulating him and telling him that he was not the world's worst signer. At the NAD office he often said, "No matter what I said, do what I mean."

There are two things that Fred was not too successful at. They were trying to find his contact lenses when they fell out and trying to grow things in his garden. I was told he always had a bumper crop of weeds. Fred moved from a printing job to a white-collar job and because of this he was always indifferent to his clothes. Bob Sanderson, who was President when Fred became Executive Secretary, once told me that if you put a new suit on Fred he will ruin it! Too many things were more important to Fred than the color of his tie. The NAD home office never got around to getting him a tie closet so he would have the opportunity to be well-coordinated color-wise.

Fred had a rare ability to make people feel good about themselves. Letters that went out from the home office to various people shone with that kind of warmth and humanity.

In closing I would like to read the statement that NAD sent out last Friday:

> Deaf people of America have lost one of their greatest advocates in the person of Frederick C. Schreiber. He was one of America's greatest humanitarians, and in this role he led the march towards full citizenship for all deaf people in this country and abroad. His dynamic leadership in building the NAD, of which he served as Executive Director, to its place as the leading national consumer organization in this country for deaf people is a monument to his ability and to the community he served.

—Ralph White

Eleanor Roosevelt once said that life was meant to be lived and curiosity must be kept alive. One never, for whatever reason, must never turn his back on life. The Fred Schreiber that hundreds and thousands and maybe millions of people with all types of disabilities knew was a man who met life straight on. Who believed that that was the only way in which problems for all people with disabilities were going to be solved. He had curiosity that stimulated everybody around him and God knows he lived life at its fullest. When we started the ACCD, Fred was there. Oh yes, he was the guidance person, and the counselor, and the father image, and the example, and a flirt once in a while. Because there were lots of us women around who ranged between 25 and 40 (that we'd admit to) and Fred would take us all under his two wide wings and try to counsel us in terms of how this new organization should go. And yes I'm sure I learned much, and Judy learned much, and Alan learned much. (But they could speak sign language and I couldn't, never did.)

More than all that we all felt that Fred was a reasonable man, a man of conviction and a man of belief, a man with whom we could have nifty fights. And we did at those ACCD Board meetings and the hands flew and the mouths went but the cause was there and we were going to have a civil rights organization that would speak for all people and Fred was going to make damn sure that that happened and it did.

On a Wednesday morning in April two years ago we proceeded to have a demonstration, a march from Capitol Hill to H.E.W. My plane from

New York was late and when I arrived about one o'clock I was greeted by a couple of the young kids from Gallaudet College who swooped me out of the cab and rushed me inside and the next thing I knew I was being walked through the crowd. An arm grabbed out for me, a voice said "Eunice" and a mustache tickled me on my cheek and I knew it was Fred. And he said "Here's a desk, jump up on it!" I was President of ACCD then and he said "Jump up on it, those people are waiting for you to lead them."

That night with Fred again as our counselor and as a guide we decided that we were going to take over the halls of H.E.W. or at least the Secretary's office. And Fred was there and we sang songs and we did all the things that kids and people in demonstrations were supposed to do. At about one o'clock in the morning Fred reached over to me and said, "Peter Libassi (who was then the general counsel to Secretary Califano) has been sent here because they're scared something's going to happen to us disabled people with these cops all around us. We ought to do something."

Fred and I said, "What are we going to do?"

And Fred said, "We've got to keep him up all night long so he's going to be as dead tomorrow as we are."

So I sent word through a guard that we wanted to see Mr. Libassi. Fred said to us, "The trick is to keep asking him all kinds of questions and get as technical as you want about 504."

And we did, until about five o'clock in the morning or five-thirty, at which time Peter Libassi finally looked at us and said, "I know what the hell you guys have done to me!"

And Fred kind of put his arm down on his knee and giggled and said, "Yes, and you're going to be right there as bleary-eyed tomorrow as we're going to be."

But Fred wasn't bleary-eyed. When we had to fight over donuts and coffee he was right there in the negotiations. When we went into secret meetings and out of secret meetings, he was right there. And when we marched out in dignity, because it was our lives and Fred's counsel, Fred was right there. And when 504 was really signed a month later, Fred was there, not only representing and always speaking for deaf people but always speaking for and about all this country's disabled people.

Fred was an example, that's true. Fred taught us many things, that's also true. Fred was also a great big tease to many of us, and I'm sure each of you has a specific memory of Fred. Let me just recount one that was very funny. Fred and I would get into some marvelous scraps, always knowing that I had somebody who would respect my position though he may or may not agree. Sometimes he would egg me on to see me get very emotional and riled up about something. One day we were leaving this campus and I forget why I was here but he was taking me somewhere. I was sitting in the front seat of his car. As you recall I do not use sign language. Fred did read some lips, but often people have some trouble reading my lips for whatever reason. But we got into some fight in the car about something. All I remember is riding down the street, Fred screaming at me, I'm screaming at him, his hands flying off the wheel and me with my background Catholic training going like this crossing herself thinking, My God, we're going to have an accident! I could hardly get in a word. He didn't know what I was saying and we went on this way for ten minutes. The car stopped, he got out, opened his side of the door, and I thought, Eunice, you're a fool; what were you arguing about? He doesn't know what you're arguing about. He got out his side, opened my door, took my arm, and as Fred would only do, with a twinkle in his eye even I could see, put his arm around me and said, "God, that was the best fight I ever had with you!"

We will all have special memories of Fred that we will cherish. We will all feel his passing deeply. But we all knew Fred and his love of life and the cause to make all people free. Fred if he were here would stomp his foot and say, "If you loved me, you must go on." Yes, we have lost a friend. But 35 million disabled people in this country will have more reason to fight for the cause, because a man in death gave love to all of us. With the rose that I will place in the vase, I will do so with the thanks and appreciation of every person with a disability in this country. Thanks for a job that was nifty and neat, that Fred did with us and with the hope that each of you will take that love and that beautiful rose and make your dedication for tomorrow, to continue the cause of love.

—Eunice Fiorito

On behalf of the World Federation of the Deaf, I have the sad obligation to say farewell to Dr. Frederick Schreiber, Executive Director of NAD, and at the same time to show proper respect to him; to the one who was the most famous man of the NAD in today's America. This obligation is even more painful for me personally because I have known him for many years, worked with him, and respected him for his enormous contribution to opening many opportunities for the deaf, not only in the United States, but also all over the world, together with the WFD.

Dr. Frederick Schreiber, with a striking visionary personality, and also being deaf himself, was engaged in solving many actual problems of the deaf people with his talent and capability. He has created faith in deaf people for their own capabilities, trying to make space and conditions for the benefit of future generations. He has succeeded, together with his associates, to develop the National Association of the Deaf into a powerful and influential organization which is highly respected now, and whose experience is valuable to many organizations of the deaf throughout the world. We know that he has always been in the front line when necessary to solve problems, that he had understanding and a sense of humanity for the needs of the deaf people. He gave unstintingly of himself, burning out slowly while doing a great and responsible job. He accepted invitations to convey his great experience to the faraway places of the world, simultaneously acquiring new knowledge about the capabilities of the deaf. We who knew him have respected his activity greatly and still remember his great contribution to the organization of the Seventh World Congress of the World Federation of the Deaf, here in Washington, in 1975.

Dr. Frederick Schreiber is no longer physically with us, but the deeds that he left behind oblige us to keep working with more persistence in creating better conditions in the field of education and training of the deaf to take their rightful place in society. We are proud for having him as a friend and associate and this is obliging us to keep permanently a memory of him and his work as we continue with our own.

The deaf of the world envy you for having such a man as Dr. Schreiber and join with me in saying to you, "Thank you for having shared him with us."

—Dragoljub Vukotic

Fred would not want this to be a time of emptiness and sorrow but a joyful day. It's a time for us all to be grateful that we had the chance to know this man . . . to share a small part of our lives with him. It's a time to go back and reminisce, to recall experiences we have shared together, in business, travel, and play. A time of laughter, heavy thought, disagreement, and maybe tears, but years that were full and filled with meaning.

Fred was a king among men, and yet one of us. With his often rumpled suit and shirt collar askew he remained a very basic person without pretense of any kind. Fred would go to fancy meetings with the top echelons of government and society in the same clothes he would rub elbows with the dishwasher at the hotel or the janitor at the club.

Fred cared deeply about many things. This included Gallaudet College which he loved, not with a blind loyalty which is sometimes superficial, but with the kind of mature love that permitted objectivity and constructive criticism. He first came to this campus as a young kid of 15 or 16 and grew to manhood on Kendall Green. For him Gallaudet provided the crucial period when the adolescent became the adult. He came to college with a lollipop and left with a cigarette instead. He used to tell me the campus was filled with meaning and memories.

Fred and I began working together when he joined the NAD Board fifteen years ago. He has left me a legacy of personal recollections which are endless, our trips to Warsaw, Rome, Paris, Copenhagen, and all of the other great cities, both in the United States and abroad.

Fred was something of a headache as a roommate. Frequently I had to follow him around picking up everything after him. He was too busy living and thinking and relating to people to be neat and orderly. I still remember Fred buying Polish money on the black market to pay off the hotel bill of the NAD tour party in Poland when we learned the travel agent had absconded with the money. I remember him in the same city trying to "rescue" us from attractive Polish professional women who were interested in our American dollars.

I recall the Centennial Committee meeting last year when we discussed expected attendance. Fred thought we were crazy to plan on a 5,000 figure and stated, and in fact signed a paper to the effect that, he would do a public striptease if we reached that magic number. As Fred watches from his throne up there in the sky I wonder what he's going to say to that broken promise.

Fred had strong feelings about young people, the Junior NAD, and its potential for youth. He did not always agree with us adults and our plans for the organization but he believed in the concept. Along with the Junior NAD he cared deeply about the NAD itself, our government, his wife and family, words, songs, and poems. For all of us he was grandfather, father, husband, leader, and friend.

In closing, as I place this red rose in the vase to symbolize each new sun, I'd like to adapt a line from the Nobel Prize Spanish poet, Juan Ramon Jimenez: You, Fred, are alone in the past. But what do you care about the past, you who live in timelessness, you who hold in your possession, as we do here, the sun of each new dawn, red as the heart of the eternal God.

—*Mervin Garretson*

My name is Sandy Ewan and I am a President of Metropolitan Washington Association of the Deaf (MWAD).

Fred is a truly All American Deaf Leader because he is a jolly person and is a winner, too. He would not give up for any deaf organization until he got what he wants for them. He will see it getting well and stronger than ever.

Fred loved to give his most time to D.C.C.D. and M.W.A.D. members and friends. D.C.C.D. stands for District of Columbia Club for the Deaf and M.W.A.D. stands for Metropolitan Washington Association for the Deaf. He held many offices for them. He was a Basketball Manager, Athletic Director, Social Director, Board Member, Secretary and President. Also, he was a founder of Dee Cee Eyes. He was fatherly to all of us, the members. We will miss you, Fred, a lot but we will not fail you, Fred. You told us, the members, last January and I will keep the members and friends thinking positively for MWAD and other deaf organizations.

Fred was the only person who gave me bright ideas to save MWAD from falling down and I took his good advice and our organization is getting stronger and stronger every week ever since.

I quoted Fred's famous saying: "If the members leave, quit or lose from any deaf organization and we will suffer more later on. And be sure to keep your head thinking positive, happy, well."

I, myself want to thank you for your helping hand with me and my organization and members. You deserve it one more time. We will watch your mother, your lovely wife, Kit, Beverly, Buddy, Bobby, Beth and three grandchildren, too.

Fred does not like for anyone crying, angry, fighting, depressed for losing people. He usually says go up for better side and cheer up for happiness.

We will meet you, Fred, again shortly.

Many thanks for inspiring me and the MWAD members and friends.

—Alexander Ewan

Frederick C. Schreiber was a master builder. Not a builder of wood and stone structures, but of organizations. He brought people together for the good of the community. He built houses of people, for people.

The list of organizations with which his name is associated is long: beginning with DCAD, we can add NAD, IAPD, ACCD, WFD, DEAF, Inc., Deaf Pride, and most recently DCA. Please forgive me if the list is far from complete. What you need to remember now is that Fred never forgot you in his lifetime. He never ignored your requests for help. Once he joined your organization he always found time to contribute to it.

Sometimes Fred was an architect, designing the structure. He understood what the poet meant when he said, "Too low they build, who build beneath the stars." Fred thought large thoughts. His were great dreams.

Sometimes Fred was the engineer. He brilliantly directed workers to carry out a plan.

Fred also could pick up a hammer and go to work himself. He was a man without false pride. He was never afraid of labor, whether with his hands or his mind. Those who toiled to build organizations were often surprised, and pleased, to find Fred working along with them at small tasks as well as large ones.

Whether his role in an organization was large or small, when he joined it, it grew! In size, in authority, in prestige. When Fred was in the group good things happened. He brought original perspectives, great energy, inspiration, and, above all, wonderful humor. His jokes were often bad, but the humor was warm and encouraging. At the darkest moment, his laughter brought courage to continue the work.

Fred leaves many building plans. In his last "Home Office Notes," written a few months ago, he discusses new publications, a credit union, the NAD Centennial, and his biggest dream—the Mutual Alliance Plan. So many blueprints for us to follow.

146

Why did Fred work so hard for others? Why was he always sacrificing his pleasure, his comfort, even his health? A few lines of poetry seem to answer well:

This chasm that has been as naught to me
To that fair-haired youth may a pitfall be;
He, too, must cross in the twilight dim,
Good friend, I am building this bridge for him.

One thing Fred was not. He was not a destroyer of people. He fought hard, he argued vigorously, but always about ideas. He never disliked enough to want to hurt. He never sought revenge, no matter how unfairly he had been attacked. He fought for others, long and bravely, never for himself. He knew the awful truth: a structure that may take years to create can be destroyed in a minute. To the last, Fred Schreiber was a builder.

Please permit me to close on a personal note. In his famous funeral oration, Marc Antony says of Caesar what I think all of us who knew Fred would like to say:

"He was my friend, faithful and just to me . . ."

—*Jerome D. Schein*

It is not easy to condense 39 years of close and privileged personal friendship into a few moments of talking with you. I am trying—and I hope each of you is able to do the same—to control my grief by reflecting on the legacies which Fred has left with us . . . not the least of which is the love that he had for us all. This generated love for him in return and by the very nature of that shared love we could not help but learn to love each other a little more. This was most typical of his life in that, in most ways, his leadership qualities were evidenced more by example than by precept. Fred often said, "If I can't take it with me, I ain't going." He was wrong, for he left us love. His love of reading was legendary. During college days, he ran out of things to read in the college library and most afternoons he could be found in Doc Harmon's Drug Store down on the corner reading the comic books. He always said that he learned more from comic books than he ever did from his college texts, things that were to be of practical value.

He found humor in most everything and was fond of other people's quips, while contributing many of his own. He loved to talk—to anyone, any time, anywhere. Even more, he loved to listen, and this was one of the traits which endeared him to us. He was very democratic and always believed that even when we disagreed with him that we had a right to our own *wrong* opinion.

Fred abhorred the traditional putdown of deaf persons and never stopped in his efforts to eradicate the stigma attached to deafness and the

147

paternalism which traditionally has been the burden of deaf persons all over the world. He had a short fuse and would blow his stack in the face of blatant discrimination. However, his anger was always short-lived and he was incapable of carrying a grudge. Fred hated any kind of class distinction or putting of people into categories. But he also told me years ago, there are three classes of people: those who make things happen, those who watch things happen, and those who wonder what happened. He was forever trying to eliminate the last two groups by setting an example himself, and then talking others of us into following his lead. I have never known anyone as adept as Fred at talking people into helping themselves by helping him. In this way, he was able continuously to make full use of his incredibly creative mind, start things rolling, and be able to move on to other and more challenging projects, knowing that he had convinced others of the benefits of carrying on what he had started.

There is no time today to enumerate all the many things that he began or hoped to begin. He did not confine his thinking and efforts either to the deaf or to the United States. That already has been documented. It needs to be pointed out, however, that throughout all this activity, he was first of all a family man, and he and Kit raised these four beautiful children.

The good book says, "Greater love hath no man than this: that he lay down his life for his friend." Fred was your friend and mine. He literally gave his life for us. Let us put aside our grief and with a smile and a quip, as Fred would want, allow the love that he left to us inspire us to carry on with the work he would want us to do.

—*Edward C. Carney*

The following tribute was not delivered at the memorial service, but it is too moving to omit.

The passing away of Fred Schreiber was mourned by thousands whose lives were touched by this great man. At the memorial service, a rose was placed in a vase for each of the many facets of Fred: as a father, a friend, a deaf leader, a helper of organizations, a world leader, a national leader, a local leader, and a leader for all disabled people. But one rose was missing. That is the rose which represents the children—deaf and hearing—who never knew him personally but whose lives have been and will continue to be changed because he cared very much about them and helped to improve their lives.

As individuals, we parents, who knew him personally, grew to love him for his tireless efforts on behalf of our children. Never before had we had someone who was not a parent of a deaf child, fight, side-by-side, with us in our fight for our children's rights to communicate and be educated. Fred did. He never waivered. One of his favorite expressions was "We are your deaf children grown." When injustices occurred, Fred was there to fight. When meetings were held, or in the planning stages, where parent input was vital, Fred made sure that we were there. His persistence in spite of adversity, to launch and sustain a national parent organization was a phenomenal effort. His encouragement, guidance and tutoring every step of the way proved to be the inspiration and motivation we needed to make the parent organization a true advocacy group.

Without Fred, would our children have the opportunity today to communicate freely at home, at school and on the street? Would they have that certain pride they have in being deaf? Would we, parents, have dared take that first step alone to help them?

Our children reap the benefits of Fred's unselfish efforts daily and yet they don't even know who was responsible for their freedom. But we know and we thank him for getting us through our darkest hours and we publicly thank him for our children.

Therefore, I place this rose for the children of today and the children of tomorrow whose lives he touched and changed; for our children who will gain strength and leadership from his efforts to become the leaders of tomorrow.

Fred left our children a legacy. He gave our children a *deaf hero*. He gave them a deaf person they could learn about: through his work, his unselfish efforts, his accomplishments, his pain, and his never-ending good humor. They can attempt to emulate and aspire to his greatness.

This rose is then to the memory of Frederick C. Schreiber, deaf hero, for the children ... the deaf children and their hearing brothers and sisters whose lives were changed because Fred cared enough to break through that communication barrier between deaf adults and hearing parents of deaf children.

—Mary Ann Locke

Fred's four children—Beverly, Elizabeth, Louis and Stephen—gathered on stage with some of those who considered themselves members of the family: Pamela Gunther, Robin Efros, Liz DeMarco, Judy Schreiber, Kathy Schreiber, James, Terri and Toni Perrell, and Robert Love. Together, the group sang a version of the popular song, "My Way," with the refrain changed to "He did it his way." Beth spoke for the family; the last rose was then presented to Kathleen Schreiber. To close the service, the family requested that the noted mime and actor, Bernard Bragg, read a poem. Mr. Bragg read Kipling's "If."

Mr. Jordan then said, "The vase—and our hearts—is almost full. Another great leader of minorities, Martin Luther King, Jr., once said: 'The ultimate measure of a man is not where he stands in moments of comfort and convenience, but where he stands at times of challenge and controversy.' Let us rejoice that we have known such a man."